Living with the
End·in·Sight

Living with the
End·in·Sight

Meditations on the Book of Revelation

Kendell · Easley
featuring the Holman Christian Standard Bible™

HOLMAN
BIBLE PUBLISHERS

Living with the End in Sight
© Copyright 2000 Holman Bible Publishers, Nashville, Tennessee
All Rights Reserved

ISBN 0-58640-001-0
Dewey Decimal Classification: 228.06
Subject Heading: N.T. Revelation

Cover and interior angel art: detail from *The Last Judgement* by Peter von
Cornelius. Courtesy of Von der Mülbe/ARTOTHEK. Used by permission.

Library of Congress Cataloging-in-Publication Data
Easley, Kendell H., 1949–
    Living with the end in sight: meditations from the book of Revelation /
Kendell H. Easley.
        p. cm.
    Inclused bibliographical references.
    ISBN 0–58640–001–0 (alk paper)
        1. Bible. N.T. Revelation—Meditations. I. Title
BS2825.4.E37   2000
228'.06—dc21   00–028949

Printed in the United States of America
2 3 4 02 01 00

Contents

Illustrations

The Holman Christian Standard Bible

Bible study is the road God's people take to hear and obey their Creator and Savior. The Holman Christian Standard Bible™ offers believers living in the third millennium an up-to-date translation designed specifically for the needs of those who study the Scriptures. It seeks to provide a translation that remains as close to the words of the Hebrew and Greek texts as possible but that also maintains a literary quality and ease of reading that invite and enable people to read, study, and obey God's Word. To reach God's people effectively, a translation must provide a reverent text that is also within its readers' grasp.

Precision With Clarity

Producing an English Bible translation offers a double challenge. First, any language has its own vocabulary, grammar, and syntax that cannot be rendered exactly into another language. This means that English translators must avoid creating a special form of the language that does not communicate well to modern readers. In Greek, for example, John 1:6 reads, "was a man having been sent from God, name to him John." The English translator must provide a word order and syntax that follow the dynamics of the English language and are familiar to English readers. In this instance, the Holman Christian Standard Bible reads, "There was a man named John who was sent from God." This accurately represents the Greek text but also presents it in a form most readers will find inviting and natural.

On the other hand, the Holman Christian Standard Bible is not based on a theory of translation that considers the form of the original language completely dispensable. Rules governing word order are very different in Hebrew, Greek, and English. However, English shares many linguistic forms with Hebrew and Greek, and in most cases these forms have similar functions in both English and the original biblical language. Therefore, since linguistic form is one way that language communicates, we have retained the original form whenever it can be translated into English with sufficient accuracy and clarity. But since it is often impossible to translate one and only one English word for every Hebrew or Greek word, this is not a strict word-for-word translation. Language differences often require several English words to translate one Hebrew or Greek word, and sometimes a Hebrew or Greek phrase may be more accurately and clearly translated by one word in English.

Communicating With Authority

The second challenge in producing an English Bible translation is that contemporary culture so honors relativism and individual freedom, it naturally distrusts claims to absolute authority. This challenge makes it important for translators to hold firmly to traditional beliefs about the authority of Scripture and to avoid the temptation to rewrite the Bible to say what some modern readers want to hear. Translators must remember that the divine Author of the Bible inspired His Word not only for the original audience, but for people of all times, including today. The Holman Christian Standard Bible holds to the authority of God's Word. It has also attempted to provide an accurate and readable translation of the Hebrew, Aramaic, and Greek Scriptures by using newly-published lexicons and grammars, as well as specialized computer programs. The goal of this kind of translation is to encourage in-depth Bible study, but this particular translation also seeks to be highly readable (for public and private use) and helpful for personal memorization.

The Makings of a New Translation

With these goals in view, an international and interdenominational team of more than eighty scholars has been formed to translate the Scriptures from the original languages. This translation project is being undertaken by Holman Bible Publishers, the oldest Bible publisher in America. Holman's origin can be traced back to a Philadelphia firm founded by Christopher Sower in 1743. The company is spiritually grounded in the belief that the Bible is inerrant and is the sole authority for faith and practice in the life of a Christian.

In order to produce this translation, Holman Bible Publishers entered into a partnership with Dr. Art Farstad, former General Editor of the New King James Version. Dr. Farstad had already been working on a new translation of the Bible for several years when, in the Spring of 1998, he contracted with Holman to complete the project. He served as General Editor of this translation project until his death on September 1, 1998. His Assistant Editor and co-worker, Dr. Ed Blum, former professor at Dallas Theological Seminary, took up the mantle of leadership and now serves as General Editor of the Holman Christian Standard Bible.

How to Enjoy This Edition

Living with the End in Sight provides an opportunity to explore the book of Revelation in the Holman Christian Standard Bible, and to enjoy a unique devotional experience as seen through Revelation's inspiring themes and graphic prophecies. Each chapter is preceded by a meditation from author and New Testament scholar Kendell Easley, offering many ways to show how the lessons of the end times apply to the here and now.

In the Bible text that follows each meditation, you'll find a brief preview of the chapter's content. Bold words and phrases within the text refer to "Living Insights" study notes that appear on the page, as well as to word studies that explain the meanings of specific Greek words and how they are used in Revelation.

The result is a Bible study with the warmth of a devotional, and a devotional with the depth of a Bible study. You'll glean encouragement from the unquestioned truths of Revelation while recognizing the different ways it is interpreted. You'll step away from the experience feeling the same way John hoped his original readers would: thoroughly convinced that, though life is hard, God is in control, and that His Word will prove true in the end.

How Do You Picture Jesus?

REVELATION 1

Christian artists throughout the centuries have been unable to avoid the urge to portray what Jesus looked like. Often, not surprisingly, paintings and sculptures reflect the culture, class, and ethnic identity of the artist rather than Jesus. One of the most popular twentieth-century American representations shows Him as a pale Scandinavian-looking person. African Christians have represented Him as black. My own favorite is by one of the great Dutch masters, Rembrandt. He shows a young olive-skinned Jewish man, only half-emerging from the shadows.

Michael Green, in his book *Who Is This Jesus?*, includes a suggestion as to what Jesus might actually have looked like: "He was a Palestinian Jew, and, as such, the color of His skin would have been olive, His eyes brown, and His nose hooked. Palestinian Jews had black hair and usually wore it long and carefully groomed. They valued a full beard, and it appears on many of the coins of the day. He wore a sleeveless undergarment with a girdle, the customary cloak and sandals, and carried a staff on journeys. That is all we know about His appearance or can guess with confidence.

"But the Bible has no interest in these things. It seems profoundly disinterested in His size, the color of His eyes and hair, and even His age and strength. These external things are unimportant. What a man is like stems from his character. And here the Bible is eloquent."

So as you read the Book of Revelation, instead of being overly concerned about Jesus' physical appearance, focus on the symbolic vision of Jesus, beginning right here in the first chapter. Consider these things:

- You'll gain little spiritual benefit from observing that Jesus was a Palestinian Jew and therefore probably had olive skin. But you'll gain great spiritual benefit from observing that He stands among the churches, present with His people to help them in their time of need.

- You'll gain little benefit from speculating that He probably had dark brown eyes, but you'll be enriched by observing that His robe and golden sash symbolize His role as our High Priest, standing in our stead before God in heaven.

- You'll gain little benefit from suggesting that He probably had long black hair and a beard, but you'll be encouraged by knowing that His white hair suggests His complete wisdom and knowledge, His blazing eyes suggest His presence everywhere at all times, and His glowing feet suggest His all-surpassing power.

Revelation may not satisfy your curiosity concerning Jesus' outward appearance, but it provides all the hope and encouragement you need by showing you through silent yet eloquent symbols who He really is. Take a good look. And stand in awe of what you see.

Prayer

*Lord Jesus, as I begin to study the Book of Revelation,
help me to see You more clearly. I praise You as the exalted
Lord, present now and forever among Your people.*

Chapter 1

Preview

The exalted Lord Jesus, walking spiritually among His churches, gives John a revelation of Himself that affirms the certainty of His glorious return.

The revelation of Jesus Christ that God gave Him to show His slaves what must quickly take place. He sent it and signified it through His angel to His slave John, ² who testified to God's word and to the testimony about Jesus Christ, in all he saw. ³ Blessed is the one who reads and blessed are those who hear the words of this prophecy and **keep what is written** in it, because **the time is near**!

⁴ John:

To the seven churches in the province of Asia.

Grace and peace to you from the One who is, who was, and who is coming; from the seven spirits before His throne; ⁵ and from Jesus Christ, the faithful witness, the firstborn from the dead and the ruler of the kings of the earth.

To Him who loves us and has set us free from our sins by His blood, ⁶ and made us a **kingdom, priests** to His God and Father—to Him be the glory and dominion forever and ever. Amen.

⁷ LOOK! HE IS COMING WITH THE CLOUDS,
and EVERY EYE WILL SEE HIM,
INCLUDING THOSE WHO PIERCED HIM.
AND ALL THE FAMILIES OF THE EARTH
WILL MOURN OVER HIM.
This is certain! Amen!

Living Insights

"keep what is written"
Revelation is more about giving us the hope to endure hardship than about pinning the tail on the Antichrist.

"the time is near"
With God, a thousand years is only a day (2 Pt 3:8). So if these events don't occur for thousands of years, they'll still be soon in God's book.

"kingdom, priests"
This is not a specialized clergy class. This is you—and anyone who claims Christ as Lord.

"tribulation"
John assumes tribulation to be the common experience of all believers.

"Son of Man"
This is Jesus' favorite title for Himself in John's Gospel. There's no question that the person John sees in his vision is Christ.

"death and Hades"
"Hades" never appears without "death" in Revelation. Watch for Jesus to destroy them both together—forever.

8 "I am the Alpha and the Omega," says the Lord God, "the One who is, who was, and who is coming, the **Almighty**."

9 I, John, your brother and partner in the **tribulation,** kingdom, and perseverance in Jesus, was on the island called Patmos because of God's word and the testimony about Jesus. 10 I was in the Spirit on the Lord's day, and I heard behind me a loud voice like a trumpet 11 saying, "Write on a scroll what you see and send it to the seven churches: Ephesus, Smyrna, Pergamum, Thyatira, Sardis, Philadelphia, and Laodicea."

12 I turned to see the voice that was speaking to me. When I turned I saw seven gold lampstands, 13 and among the lampstands was One like the **Son of Man,** dressed in a long robe, and with a gold sash wrapped around His chest. 14 His head and hair were white like wool—white as snow, His eyes like a fiery flame, 15 His feet like fine bronze fired in a furnace, and His voice like the sound of cascading waters. 16 In His right hand He had seven stars; from His mouth came a sharp two-edged sword; and His face was shining like the sun at midday.

17 When I saw Him, I fell at His feet like a dead man. He laid His right hand on me, and said, "Don't be afraid! I am the First and the Last, 18 and the Living One. I was dead, but look—I am alive forever and ever, and I hold the keys of **death and Hades.** 19 Therefore write what you have seen, what is, and what will take place after this. 20 The secret of the seven stars you saw in My right hand, and of the seven gold lampstands is this: the seven stars are the angels of the seven churches, and the seven lampstands are the seven churches.

Word Study

"Almighty"

The Greek word *pantokrator* [pahn tah KRAH tohr] comes from the word meaning *all (pan)* and the word for *might, strength,* or *power (kratos).* This word, then, means *all power* or *all strength* and is sometimes translated *omnipotent.* Nine of the ten uses of *pantokrator* in the New Testament are in Revelation, where the word always refers to God the Father. The occurrence in 1:8 is the only possible exception to this, where *pantokrator* could refer to Christ.

End-Times Insight

Make sure you know Jesus well.
And always listen to what He has to say.

Pew Sitters and Backsliders

When I was growing up in eastern Oklahoma, one of the favorite pulpit topics was backsliding. Church members regularly came forward at the end of the services, shook the preacher's hand, and stated their dedication to follow Christ more closely. I must confess, though, that as an adult, I have heard very few sermons on backsliding. I don't think the reason is that Christians are more committed now than they used to be.

Noah's message from the steps of the ark was that kind of appeal. It was hardly an "I'm OK, you're OK" sermon. Noah proclaimed, "Repent." Judah's king didn't put Jeremiah in a pit for saying that "God's in His heaven; all's right with the world." He did it because Jeremiah told the king and the people to repent. Herod didn't behead John the Baptist for teaching how to win friends and influence people, but because John told Herod to repent of his infidelity and sin. From beginning to end, the Bible reports how God's messengers called people to repent and warned them of God's judgment if they did not.

In Revelation, Jesus called the churches in Asia to repent, naming the specific sins of each congregation and warning them of approaching judgment. We don't know how any of these churches responded. But we do know that every church (including ours today) needs to hear a clear description of its sins and a clear warning of God's judgment. Revelation 2 reminds us that we, too, often tolerate these same sins and therefore face the danger of these same penalties.

For example, many suppose the church of Thyatira with its open immorality was more wicked than the church of Ephesus with its lovelessness. Wrong! The Lord demanded repentance from both sins. A church that tolerates spiritual coldness must exercise the same repentance required of a church that tolerates outright immorality. In God's eyes sins of the flesh and sins of the spirit are equally vile and therefore worthy of judgment.

Certainly, some acts are morally evil in any circumstance. Sexual behavior outside of marriage, for instance, always offends God. Other acts are morally neutral and only become evil in particular circumstances. Christians have to be on guard in these gray areas—activities that are not outright wrong but still defile the conscience; motives that can be justified through clever argument but damage the church's witness.

How easy it is in our persistent, permissive culture to let down our guard, like the church of Thyatira, and suddenly find that we've welcomed "Jezebel" into our midst. Eternal vigilance is the price we all must pay if we and our churches are to remain doctrinally and morally pure.

Prayer

Lord Jesus, turn Your searchlight on me (and my church) just as You did on the churches of Asia. Whether sin has slipped in or has been formally invited, I want to turn away from it all.

Chapter 2

Preview

Jesus, fully knowing the strengths and weaknesses of each local church, gives both cheers and challenges to prepare them for the days ahead.

"To the angel of the church in Ephesus write:

"The One who holds the seven stars in His right hand and who walks among the seven gold lampstands says: **2** I know your works, your labor, and your endurance, and that you cannot tolerate evil. You have tested those who call themselves apostles and are not, and you have found them to be liars. **3** You also possess endurance and have tolerated many things because of My name, and have not grown weary. **4** But I have this against you: you have **lost the love** you had at first. **5** Remember then how far you have fallen, repent, and do the works you did at first. Otherwise, I will come to you and **remove your lampstand** from its place—unless you repent. **6** Yet you do have this: you hate the practices of the Nicolaitans, which I also hate.

7 "Anyone who has an ear should listen to what the Spirit says to the churches. I will give the victor the right to eat from the tree of life, which is in the paradise of God.

8 "To the angel of the church in Smyrna write:

"The First and the Last, the One who was dead and came to life, says: **9** I know your tribulation and poverty, yet you are rich. I know the slander of those who say they are Jews and are not, but are a synagogue of Satan. **10** Don't be afraid of what you are about to suffer. Look, the Devil is about to throw some of you into prison to test you, and you will have tribulation for ten days. Be **faithful until death,** and I will give you the crown of life.

11 "Anyone who has an ear should listen to what the Spirit says to the churches. The victor will never be harmed by the second death.

12 "To the angel of the church in Pergamum write:

"The One who has the sharp, two-edged sword says: **13** I know where you live—where Satan's throne is! And you are holding on to My name and did not deny your faith in Me, even in the days of Antipas, My faithful witness, who was killed among you, where Satan lives. **14** But I have a few things against you. You have some there who hold to the teaching of Balaam, who taught Balak to place a stumbling block in front of the sons of Israel: to eat meat sacrificed to idols and to commit sexual immorality. **15** In the same way, you also have those who hold to the teaching of the Nicolaitans. **16** Therefore repent! Otherwise, I will come to you quickly and fight against them with the sword of My mouth.

17 "Anyone who has an ear should listen to what the Spirit says to the churches. I will give **the victor** some of the hidden manna. I will also give him a **white stone,** and on the stone a new name is inscribed that no one knows except the one who receives it.

18 "To the angel of the church in Thyatira, write:

"The Son of God, the One whose eyes are like a fiery flame, and whose feet are like fine bronze says: **19** I know your works—your love, faithfulness, service, and endurance.

Word Study
"Victor"

The Greek verb *nikao* [nih KAH oh] means *to conquer*, and the related noun *nike* [nih KAY] means *victory*. *Nikao* was a common term used to describe various aspects of warfare. The word was also used as a legal term for winning a case. In the New Testament, *nikao* refers to actual warfare only in Revelation (6:2; 11:7; 13:7; 17:14); elsewhere it is used figuratively. Each of the seven messages in chapters two and three ends with a promise to "the victor."

Living Insights

"lost the love"
Right doctrine without a right heart leads to a theology that's as clear as ice, but just about as cold.

"remove your lampstand"
Today, the Ephesian church is dead. Apparently, they didn't repent. Apparently, God meant what He said.

"faithful until death"
The early believers fully expected persecution, and never expected the Christian life to be a cakewalk.

"the victor"
The possibility of winning this conquering title gives us an indication of what Christian living really is: all-out spiritual war.

"white stone"
In the ancient world, white stones were used as admission tickets to public festivals. But this one gets people into heavenly places.

"Jezebel"
She was like those today who incorporate pagan practices into the Christian life, all in the name of tolerance and personal freedom.

Your last works are greater than the first. **20** But I have this against you: you tolerate the woman **Jezebel**, who calls herself a prophetess, and teaches and deceives My slaves to commit sexual immorality and to eat meat sacrificed to idols. **21** I gave her time to repent, but she does not want to repent of her sexual immorality. **22** Look! I will throw her into a sickbed, and those who commit adultery with her into great tribulation, unless they repent of her practices. **23** I will kill her children with the plague. Then all the churches will know that I am the One who examines minds and hearts, and I will give to each of you according to your works. **24** I say to the rest of you in Thyatira, who do not hold this teaching, who haven't known the deep things of Satan—as they say—I do not put any other burden on you. **25** But hold on to what you have until I come. **26** The victor and the one who keeps My works to the end: I will give him authority over the nations—

> **27** AND HE WILL SHEPHERD THEM WITH AN IRON SCEPTER;
>   HE WILL SHATTER THEM LIKE POTTERY—

just as I have received this from My Father. **28** I will also give him the morning star.

29 "Anyone who has an ear should listen to what the Spirit says to the churches.

End-Times Insight

Keep your heart clean, your motives pure. And invigorate them each day in the refreshing waters of repentance.

Your Name Here

In the blockbuster movie *Titanic*, the fictional character Jack Dawson wins a ticket for passage to New York in a dockside card game just before the ship sails. His elation skyrockets as his dream of returning home to America now seems days—not years, not a lifetime—away. Finally, he can cast his drifting ways into the forgiving wake of an unbelievable promise—a new day filled with hope and excitement, with new beginnings and fresh opportunities.

Then tragedy strikes. What appeared to be a ticket to complete fulfillment has turned into a reservation with death in the icy North Atlantic.

Yes, the *Titanic* had promised safe delivery to all its passengers, from first class all the way down to standard fare. But more of them drowned than survived. Not all promises are what they appear, and this promise of unsinkable safety had proven drastically false.

But there is a divine list of passengers bound for heaven, and all who are on God's list will undoubtedly reach their destination. How do we know? God says their names are already written in the Lamb's book of life.

The first biblical mention we find of such a divine ledger is in Exodus 32:32–33, where God informs Moses that He will blot out of His book those who continue to sin against Him. This idea of a book of life continues to surface in other Old Testament waters, such as David's appeal in Psalm 69:28 that God strike the name of the sinful from the book of the living, and Daniel's stirring encouragement from Daniel 12:1 that those whose names are written in the book of life will be delivered from the fiery jaws of persecution and calamity.

In Revelation, however, this concept of a book of life develops in greater detail (chapters 3, 13, 17, 20, and 21).

In ancient cities, a scroll like the one mentioned in Revelation was used as a register of all the citizens, similar perhaps to the printouts of registered voters you see in American precincts each election day. To have one's name erased from this book would indicate a loss of citizenship.

But God is not striking names from His registry—those names that have been "written in the book of life from the foundation of the world" (Rv 17:8). He is not constantly reaching for the eraser, but is preparing a place for those whose names are "written in the Lamb's book of life" (Rv 21:27). The blessings of eternal life await us over on the other shore. And if you're one of those believing souls who has put your trust in Him, His grace will be sure to keep you afloat.

Prayer

*Lord, I thank You for writing my name in Your book, not because
I deserve to be there, but because You desire me to be with You.
Help me to live my life in gratitude for Your graciousness.*

Chapter 3

Preview

Jesus continues both to compliment and confront the churches of Asia Minor, declaring His expectations while always extending His eternal promises.

"To the angel of the church in Sardis, write:

"The One who has the seven spirits of God and the seven stars says: **I know your works;** you have a reputation for being alive, but you are dead. **2** Be alert and strengthen what remains, which is about to die, for I have not found your works complete before My God. **3** Remember therefore what you have received and heard; keep it, and repent. But if you are not alert, I will come like a thief, and you have no idea at what hour I will come against you. **4** But you have **a few people** in Sardis who have not defiled their clothes, and they will walk with me in white, because they are worthy. **5** In the same way, the victor will be dressed in white clothes, and I will never erase his name from the book of life, but will acknowledge his name before My Father and before His angels.

6 "Anyone who has an ear should listen to what the Spirit says to the churches.

7 "To the angel of the church in Philadelphia write:

"The Holy One, the True One, the One who has the key of David, who opens and no one will close, and closes and no one opens says: **8** I know your works. Look, I have placed before you an open door that no one is able to close; because you have limited strength, have kept My word, and have not denied My name. **9** Take note! I will make those from the synagogue of Satan, who claim to be Jews and are not, but are lying—note this—I will make them come and bow down at your feet, and they will know that I have loved you. **10** Because you have kept My command to endure, I will also keep you from the **hour of testing** that is going to come over the whole world to test those who live on the earth. **11** I am coming quickly. Hold on to what you have, so that no one takes your crown. **12** The victor: I will make him a **pillar in the**

Word Study

"Originator"

The Greek noun *arche* [ahr KAY] is the basic New Testament term for *beginning*. It appears twice in Revelation as an exalted title for Jesus (3:14; 22:13). The latter passage uses the same phrase that describes God the Father in Revelation 21:6: "the Beginning [*arche*] and the End," the Originator and Consummator of all things. Revelation 3:14, then, verifies that the Son and the Father are one, that Jesus Himself is the Creator, "the Originator of God's creation."

sanctuary of My God, and he will never go out again. I will write on him the name of My God, and the name of the city of My God—the new Jerusalem, which comes down out of heaven from My God—and My new name.

¹³ "Anyone who has an ear should listen to what the Spirit says to the churches.

¹⁴ "To the angel of the church in Laodicea, write:

"The Amen, the faithful and true Witness, the **Originator** of God's creation says: ¹⁵ I know your works, that you are neither cold nor hot. I wish that you were cold or hot. ¹⁶ So, because you are lukewarm, and neither hot nor cold, I am going to vomit you out of My mouth. ¹⁷ Because you say, 'I'm rich; I have become wealthy, and need nothing,' and **you don't know** that you are wretched, pitiful, poor, blind, and naked, ¹⁸ I advise you to buy from Me gold refined in the fire so that you may be rich, and white clothes so that you may be dressed and your shameful nakedness not be exposed, and ointment to spread on your eyes so that you may see. ¹⁹ As many as I love, I **rebuke and discipline**. So be committed and repent. ²⁰ Listen!

Living Insights

"I know your works"
The church in Sardis may have been fooling everybody else, but Jesus sees what no one else suspects.

"a few people"
The idea of a faithful remnant of believers is a common theme in Scripture. They often go unnoticed, but by God's grace they remain unspotted by the world's corruption.

"hour of testing"
This is the first specific reference in Revelation to a coming time of worldwide upheaval—a great tribulation initiated by God.

"pillar in the sanctuary"
Philadelphia had recently been rocked by a devastating earthquake. This promise gave them an unshakable hope in God's solid promises.

"you don't know"
The only thing worse than being spiritually poor, blind, and naked is to be all three at once and not even know it.

"rebuke and discipline"
Christ's words of warning are really words of love—painful truths that help us avoid painful consequences.

I stand at the door and knock. If anyone hears My voice and opens the door, I will come in to him and have dinner with him, and he with Me. ²¹ The victor: I will give him the right to sit with Me on My throne, just as I also won the victory and sat down with My Father on His throne.

²² "Anyone who has an ear should listen to what the Spirit says to the churches."

End-Times Insight

The relief we seek through pleasure and laziness is actually found only through perseverance.

His Rightful Throne

REVELATION 4

As an American, I can't really relate to the experience of bowing before a human sovereign. The president of the United States is a fellow citizen elected by the people to serve for only a few years, and though I honor and respect his office, I also enjoy the privilege of speaking my mind and holding him accountable to his sworn oath.

Yet for the ancient peoples reading or hearing the book of Revelation for the first time, bowing before the king was a very natural reaction. Only with the rise of modern democracies have kings and their thrones become largely relics of symbolic power. To earlier peoples, the throne still meant something. It meant strength and superiority and a monarch to be revered (albeit willingly or unwillingly) by his subjects.

In more recent times, it has been the throne itself, not the power it symbolizes, that has commanded the most attention. One of the most splendid thrones in history was the jeweled Peacock Throne of India, later stolen and taken to Iran. Many European kingdoms also created elaborate thrones for their kings. The oldest throne in continuous use is a thirteenth-century carved oak chair in London's House of Lords. To this day the British monarch officially opens sessions of Parliament from this throne.

In a way, however, all human beings sit on their own individual thrones, desiring to rule their own affairs without interference from God or other people. I encountered this truth when I was a college student learning to share my faith in Christ. Near the end of the gospel presentation known as "The Four Spiritual Laws," there is a diagram with two circles. Each circle has a small chair or throne at the center. One circle shows self on the throne; the other shows Christ on the throne. In sharing this idea, I would ask people to tell me which circle represented their life, then ask which one showed the kind of life they would like to have.

Ultimately, earth knows only these two kinds of people: those who have enthroned Christ in their lives and those who have enthroned themselves. As this chapter of Revelation demonstrates, God is absolutely secure on the throne of the universe. His plan will be perfectly fulfilled. The issue we must face, then, is this: What about the throne of our own lives?

If you have acknowledged that God is your personal sovereign, thank Him for His greatness and goodness. Worship Him by reading aloud the songs of Revelation 4. But if you have not acknowledged God as your master, consider the following chapter an opportunity to reflect on your need to put Him where He rightly belongs.

Prayer

Lord, I acknowledge You not only as the Sovereign of the heavenly throne, but also as the Sovereign on the throne of my life. Help me, Lord, to pay whatever price I must in order to keep You there.

Chapter 4

Preview

The second vision of Revelation opens in the throne room of God, where heavenly worshipers are caught up in the flow of praise.

After this I looked, and there in heaven was an open door. The first voice that I had heard speaking to me like a trumpet said, "Come up here, and I will show you what **must take place** after this."

2 Immediately I was **in the Spirit**, and there in heaven a throne was set. One was seated on the throne, 3 and the One seated looked like jasper and carnelian stone. A **rainbow** that looked like an emerald surrounded the throne. 4 Around that throne were twenty-four thrones, and on the thrones sat twenty-four elders dressed in white clothes, with gold crowns on their heads. 5 From the throne came flashes of lightning, rumblings, and thunder. Burning before the throne were seven fiery torches, which are the seven spirits of God. 6 Also before the throne was something like a **sea of glass**, similar to crystal. In the middle and around the throne were four living creatures covered with eyes in front and in back. 7 The first living creature was like a lion; the second living creature was like a calf; the third living creature had a face like a man; and the fourth living creature was like a flying eagle. 8 Each of the four living creatures had six wings; they were covered with eyes around and inside. Day and night they **never stop**, saying:

Living Insights

"must take place"
There is no maybe in the coming events of Revelation. Nothing in life is more certain than God's Word.

"in the Spirit"
Revelation actually consists of four separate visions. Spot the others by looking for these same three words in 1:10, 17:3, and 21:10.

"rainbow"
The rainbow is God's eternal sign (remember Noah and the ark?) that He will never forget His covenant promise to humanity.

"sea of glass"
Oceans are usually anything but clear, just as even the finest of glass works were in John's day. This "crystal sea" certainly caught his attention.

"never stop"
We are like these heavenly beings who have no other purpose for existing. We too were created to worship God.

"Lord and God"
The wicked Roman emperor Domitian had blasphemously claimed this title for himself. The early Christians knew who really owned it.

Holy, holy, holy,
Lord God, the Almighty,
who was, who is, and who is coming.

9 Whenever the living creatures give glory, honor, and thanks to the One seated on the throne, the One who lives forever and ever, 10 the twenty-four elders fall down before the One seated on the throne, worship the One who lives forever and ever, cast their crowns before the throne and say:

11 "Our **Lord and God**,
You are worthy to receive
glory and honor and power,
because You have created all things,
and because of Your will
they exist and were created."

End-Times Insight

*Get good at worshiping.
You'll be doing it for a long time.*

Word Study
"h o l y"

The adjective *hagios* [HAH gee ahss] is related to the verb *hagiazo*, which means *to set apart*, often translated *sanctify*. The essential idea of *hagios* is *uniqueness*, that which is different from everything else. God's unique attribute of holiness is the focus of the angels' threefold chant in Revelation 4:8. The term also describes certain things that God has set apart for His own purposes, such as "the holy city" (11:2, 21:2,10) and (in its plural noun form) the "saints"—that is, Christians (5:8).

What Are We Doing Here?

REVELATION 5

One of the great tragedies produced in English drama, Shakespeare's *Macbeth*, was published in 1623. Near the play's end, Macbeth's wife dies. By this time Macbeth has so lost his conscience that he is unable to feel anything at all. He expresses his weariness in the following famous lines:

> Tomorrow, and tomorrow, and tomorrow,
> Creeps in this petty pace from day to day
> To the last syllable of recorded time;
> And all our yesterdays have lighted fools
> The way to dusty death. Out, out brief candle!
> Life's but a walking shadow, a poor player
> That struts and frets his hour upon the stage
> And then is heard no more. It is a tale
> Told by an idiot, full of sound and fury,
> Signifying nothing [*Macbeth*, act 5, scene 5].

Four centuries later, many would still argue that history has no pattern, that while it may be "full of sound and fury," it is really a noisy ride to nowhere. The Christian view, however, is that God has a script for the future of the universe. And nowhere is this seen more clearly than in Revelation 5, where the scroll appears, written on both sides. Jesus knows all about the events that have occurred and will occur between the first century and the end-time judgments—the breaking of the seals. He is also in charge of making the end-time judgments unfold according to God's plan. He is the One—the only One—found worthy to open the scroll and to look inside. This Jesus, the Lamb of God, is taking history somewhere—both to a dramatic conclusion and an eternal destiny.

We are a part of that destiny as we commit ourselves to serve in His Kingdom—as we worship and witness, as we obey His Word and do His work. We are joining with the hymn writer Matthew Bridges, who drew these words from the imagery of Revelation 5:

> Crown Him with many crowns,
> The Lamb upon His throne;
> Hark! how the heavenly anthem drowns
> All music but its own;
> Awake, my soul, and sing
> Of Him who died for thee,
> And hail Him as thy matchless King
> Through all eternity.

Prayer

Lord, I know that You are in total control of the future, just as You have been in total control of the past. I trust You to take me where You want me to go. Make me a willing follower.

Chapter 5

Preview

Declared worthy to
open the judgment
scroll of destiny,
Christ, the slaughtered
Lamb, arrives to the
glorious worship of
the heavenly court.

Then I saw in the right hand of the One seated on the throne a **scroll** with writing on the inside and on the back, sealed with seven seals. ² I also saw a mighty angel proclaiming in a loud voice, "Who is worthy to open the scroll and **break its seals?**" ³ But no one in heaven or on earth or under the earth was able to open the scroll or even to look in it. ⁴ And I cried and cried because no one was found worthy to open the scroll or even to look in it.

⁵ Then one of the elders said to me, "Stop crying. Look! The **Lion** from the tribe of Judah, the Root of David, has been victorious so that He may open the scroll and its seven seals." ⁶ Then I saw one like a slaughtered **lamb** standing between the throne and the four living creatures and among the elders. He had **seven horns** and seven eyes, which are the seven spirits of God sent into all the earth. ⁷ He came and took the scroll out of the right hand of the One seated on the throne.

⁸ When He took the scroll, the four living creatures and the twenty-four elders fell down before the Lamb. Each one had a harp and gold bowls filled with incense, which are the **prayers of the saints.** ⁹ And they sang a new song:

Living Insights

"scroll"
This is God's judgment scroll, His eternal plan to condemn wickedness.

"break its seals"
This will not yet reveal the scroll's contents. All seven seals must be broken just to see the opening edge of God's plan.

"Lion" and "lamb"
What sounds like a lion but looks like a lamb? Jesus, the conquering king of the universe, the living picture of perfect power and peace.

"seven horns"
The horns of an animal represent its power. The Lamb's seven horns, therefore, represent ultimate power.

"prayers of the saints"
Ever feel like your prayers are going nowhere? Watch them here as they rise to the throne room of heaven.

"then I looked"
Look through John's lens as he widens his view from the throne, to its guardians, to the angels, to the countless worshipers. Squint your mind's eye to see it yourself.

You are worthy to take the scroll
and to open its seals;
because You were slaughtered,
and You redeemed people for God
   by Your blood
from every tribe and language
   and people and nation.
¹⁰ You made them a kingdom and priests
   to our God,
   and they will reign on the earth.

¹¹ **Then I looked**, and heard the voice of many angels around the throne, and also of the living creatures, and of the elders. Their number was countless thousands, plus thousands of thousands. ¹² They said with a loud voice:

The Lamb who was slaughtered is worthy
to receive power and riches
and wisdom and strength
and honor and glory and blessing!

¹³ I heard every creature in heaven, on earth, under the earth, on the sea, and everything in them say:

Blessing and honor and glory and dominion
to the One seated on the throne,
and to the Lamb, forever and ever!

¹⁴ The four living creatures said, "Amen," and the elders fell down and worshiped.

Word Study
"scroll"

The Greek noun *biblion* [bihb LEE ahn] and its close relative *biblos* mean *scroll*. Both are often translated as *book*, since a document or a collection of documents is often in view (22:7). These words are basically interchangeable, as in the use of both for the "book of life" (*biblion*, 13:8; 17:8; 20:12; 21:27; *biblos*, 3:5; 20:15). The related term *biblaridion* means *little book* and occurs three times in the New Testament (10:2,9,10). These form the basis for our word *Bible*.

End-Times Insight

*Never let the dull rhythm of this day
make you think there's not an end in sight.*

The Four Horsemen

Our world is filled with unavoidable suffering. Famines, epidemics, earthquakes, floods, hurricanes, and airplane crashes inflict untold pain and loss on humanity. We have no way of counting how many have suffered or died because of such disasters.

On top of that stands man's inhumanity to man. War, terrorism, crime, domestic abuse, and discrimination heap horror upon horror. In the twentieth century, Adolf Hitler was the very picture of evil. His racist goal was to eliminate all those he considered inferior to him and create a race of supermen. In pursuit of this dreadful goal, he eliminated millions of Jews, Gypsies, Poles, Slavs, and others.

But even Hitler wasn't the worst. Joseph Stalin, the father of militant communism, murdered at least forty million of his own countrymen. Even Stalin was outdone by Mao Zedong of China. Perhaps seventy-two million Chinese perished in Chairman Mao's revolution, the effort to collectivize the country, and in the Cultural Revolution that followed.

Whenever people turn away from God, unspeakable horror results. More than a century ago, James Russell Lowell spoke at a gathering where Christianity had been questioned. He responded, "I challenge any skeptic to find a ten square mile spot on this planet where they can live their lives in peace and safety and decency, where womanhood is honored, where infancy and old age are revered, where they can educate their children, where the gospel of Jesus Christ has not gone first to prepare the way. If they find such a place, then I would encourage them to emigrate there and proclaim their unbelief" (D. James Kennedy, *What if Jesus Had Never Lived?*).

How do we respond to pain and distress? We encourage people to turn to Christ to avoid as much avoidable suffering as possible. We live with patience and perseverance and follow Christ whatever the cost. We cast ourselves headlong on the sovereignty of God without demanding an explanation for why He allows such pain to continue. We may cry out with the martyrs, "How long, O Lord?" But at the same time we affirm the goodness of God. He is all-powerful. He still rules from His heavenly throne. One day, after His wrath has been poured out fully on sin, all wrongs will be righted. Despite the suffering brought on by the four horsemen, all will be well in the end. Justice and love will ultimately prevail.

Prayer

God, You are Lord of history, even when the world seems mad with political and military disasters. You are Lord of nature, even when nature seems out of control. You are Lord. Yes—You are Lord.

Chapter 6

Preview

The terrifying ride of the four horsemen reveals an ourpouring of war, waste, death, and destruction.

Then I saw the Lamb open one of the seven **seals**, and I heard one of the four living creatures say with a voice like thunder, "Come!" **2** I looked, and there was a **white horse**. The horseman on it had a bow; a crown was given to him, and he went out as a victor to conquer.

3 When He opened the second seal, I heard the second living creature say, "Come!" **4** Then another horse went out, a fiery red one, and its horseman was empowered to take peace from the earth, so that people would slaughter one another. And a large sword was given to him.

5 When He opened the third seal, I heard the third living creature say, "Come!" And I looked, and there was a black horse. The horseman on it had a balance scale in his hand. **6** Then I heard something like a voice among the four living creatures say, "A quart of wheat for a **denarius**, and three quarts of barley for a denarius—but do not harm the olive oil and the wine."

7 When He opened the **fourth seal**, I heard the voice of the fourth living creature say, "Come!" **8** And I looked, and there was a **pale green** horse. The horseman on it was named Death, and Hades was following after him. Authority was given to them over a fourth of the earth, to kill by the sword, by famine, by plague, and by the wild animals of the earth.

Living Insights

"white horse"
Unlike the one Jesus rides in chapter 19, this white horse isn't a symbol of purity. Rather, it probably symbolizes the empty promises of peace that precede military domination.

"denarius"
This Roman coin was standard pay for a day's wages—and at these prices, hardly enough to get by on.

"fourth seal"
Four in Revelation seems to represent the world, meaning these first four seals stand for global scourges.

"pale green"
Most likely this relates to the gray-green pall of a human corpse. It's ugly any way you look at it.

"they cried out"
"Will not God grant justice to His elect who cry out to Him day and night? Will He delay to help them?" (Lk 18:7). Never give up on God.

"wrath of the Lamb"
It is fair to attribute at least some of today's cataclysmic disasters to God's anger against human sin.

⁹ When He opened the fifth seal, I saw under the altar the souls of those slaughtered because of God's word and the testimony they had. **¹⁰ They cried out** with a loud voice: "O Lord, holy and true, how long until You judge and avenge our blood from those who live on the earth?" ¹¹ So a white robe was given to each of them, and they were told to rest a little while longer until the number of their fellow slaves and their brothers, who were going to be killed just as they had been, would be completed.

¹² Then I saw Him open the sixth seal. A violent earthquake occurred; the sun turned black like sackcloth made of goat hair; the entire moon became like blood; ¹³ the stars of heaven fell to the earth as a fig tree drops its unripe figs when shaken by a high wind; ¹⁴ the sky separated like a scroll being rolled up; and every mountain and island was moved from its place.

¹⁵ Then the kings of the earth, the nobles, the military commanders, the rich, the powerful, and every slave and free person hid in the caves and among the rocks of the mountains. ¹⁶ And they said to the mountains and to the rocks, "Fall on us and hide us from the face of the One seated on the throne and from the **wrath of the Lamb**, ¹⁷ because the great day of their wrath has come! And who is able to stand?"

Word Study
" s e a l "

The noun *sphragis* [sfrah GIHSS] means *seal* or *signet*. The related verb *sphragizo* means to *seal* or *to mark with a seal*. In Revelation, these terms primarily refer to ownership. The scroll with seven seals belongs to God and can only be opened by the Lamb (chapters 5–6; 8:1). Likewise, those who have the seal of God belong to Him (7:3-8). But the theme of protection is also seen— protection *for* those *who* are sealed (9:4), protection *from* that *which* is sealed (10:4; 20:3)

E n d - T i m e s   I n s i g h t

The headlines reveal the human cost of rejecting God's love and ignoring God's grace.

Today's Tribulation

REVELATION 7

Many Christians have fretted about how the tribulation might affect them. My beloved father-in-law, Bob, was one of them. In the late 1970s he became convinced that he needed to stockpile food for the family. He didn't want us to starve to death in case of severe famine or in case Christians were forbidden to purchase anything during the coming days of crisis. He invested a substantial amount of savings into hundreds of cans of specially processed food, everything from whole-wheat flour to peanut butter to dried banana flakes. Supposedly, he gathered enough to feed us (sparingly) for three years. All the goods had a guaranteed shelf life of at least ten years.

Well, Bob died in 1982, leaving in his garage row upon row of untouched cans. Finally in 1997, they were all disposed of—a total loss. What Bob didn't understand is that tribulation must be prepared for spiritually, not physically.

The noun "tribulation" (Greek *thlipsis*) is found 43 times in the New Testament. Its basic idea is "pressure" in a negative sense. Our English word comes from the Latin *tribulum*, the harrow or threshing instrument that separates grain from its husk. In Revelation, *thlipsis* occurs five times:

- 1:9—I, John, your brother and partner in the **tribulation**, kingdom, and perseverance in Jesus, was on the island called Patmos because of God's word and the testimony about Jesus.

- 2:9—"I know your **tribulation** and poverty, yet you are rich. I know the slander of those who say they are Jews and are not, but are a synagogue of Satan."

- 2:10—"Don't be afraid of what you are about to suffer. Look, the Devil is about to throw some of you into prison to test you, and you will have **tribulation** for ten days. Be faithful until death, and I will give you the crown of life."

- 2:22—Look! I will throw her into a sickbed, and those who commit adultery with her into great **tribulation**, unless they repent of her practices.

- 7:14—I said to him, "Sir, you know." Then he told me: "These are the ones coming out of the great **tribulation**. They washed their robes and made them white in the blood of the Lamb."

Certainly, John and the Christians of his day were going through tribulation. But as God's people, we find in our Father the strength to endure our time of tribulation faithfully and with joy.

Prayer

Lord, I am willing to walk through the tribulation
You send into my life. How I look forward to being part
of the multitude that will be in Your presence forever.

Chapter 7

Preview

Suddenly, there's a break in the action, as the redeemed are shielded from destruction and sealed for all eternity.

After this I saw four angels standing at the four corners of the earth, restraining the four winds of the earth so that no wind could blow on the earth or on the sea or on any tree. **2** Then I saw another angel rise up from the east, who had the **seal of the living God**. He cried out in a loud voice to the four angels who were empowered to harm the earth and the sea: **3** "Don't harm the earth or the sea or the trees until we seal the slaves of our God on their foreheads." **4** And I heard the number of those who were sealed:

> **144,000** sealed from every tribe of the **sons of Israel**:
> **5** 12,000 sealed from the tribe of Judah,
> 12,000 from the tribe of Reuben,
> 12,000 from the tribe of Gad,
> **6** 12,000 from the tribe of Asher,
> 12,000 from the tribe of Naphtali,
> 12,000 from the tribe of Manasseh,
> **7** 12,000 from the tribe of Simeon,
> 12,000 from the tribe of Levi,
> 12,000 from the tribe of Issachar,
> **8** 12,000 from the tribe of Zebulun,
> 12,000 from the tribe of Joseph,
> 12,000 sealed from the tribe of Benjamin.

9 After this I looked, and there was a vast multitude from every nation, **tribe**, people, and language, which no one could number, standing before the throne and before the Lamb. They were robed in white with **palm branches** in their hands. **10** And they cried out in a loud voice:

> Salvation belongs to our God,
> who is seated on the throne,
> and to the Lamb!

11 All the angels stood around the throne, the elders, and the four living creatures, and they fell on their faces before the throne and worshiped God, **12** saying:

> Amen! Blessing and glory and wisdom
> and thanksgiving and honor
> and power and strength,
> be to our God forever and ever. Amen.

13 Then one of the elders asked me, "Who are these people robed in white, and where did they come from?"

14 I said to him, "Sir, you know."

Then he told me:

> These are **the ones coming** out of the
>   great tribulation.
> They washed their robes and made them
>   white
> in the blood of the Lamb.
> **15** For this reason they are before the
>   throne of God,
> and they serve Him day and night in His sanctuary.
> The One seated on the throne will shelter them:
> **16 no longer** will they hunger; no longer will they thirst;

Word Study

"tribe"

The Greek noun *phule* [foo LAY] could mean *race* but most often referred to close blood relations within a race, thus *tribe* or *clan*. Two-thirds of the occurrences of *phule* in Revelation are in chapter seven, where the twelve tribes of Israel are specifically named. The term *phule* is used of Israel's tribes in other contexts (5:5; 21:12), yet it can also refer to people of other races (1:7; 5:9; 7:9; 11:9; 13:7; 14:6) as a synonym for *genos (race)* or *ethnos (Gentile or nation).*

Living Insights

"seal of the living God"
Whether literal or not, this seal directly contrasts with the famous mark of the beast from chapter 13.

"144,000"
Though perhaps symbolic of a huge amount, this number alone would have seemed enormous to the first-century Christian.

"sons of Israel"
Just as the original tribes lived through the ten plagues of the Exodus, these tribes in the end times will survive these latter-day plagues.

"palm branches"
Palm branches were the ancient equivalent of balloons at a party, a mark of joy and festivity.

"the ones coming"
This present tense verb suggests that the saints will flow into heaven at a steady stream throughout the tribulation.

"no longer"
The elder's promise of abundant supply indicates that many of the arriving believers have suffered the very opposite of that on earth.

no longer will the sun strike them, or any heat.
¹⁷ Because the Lamb who is at the center of the throne will
    shepherd them;
He will guide them to springs of living waters,
and God will wipe away every tear from their eyes.

End-Times Insight

Expect life to be hard. But remember,
your reward will more than make up for it.

Reading Between the Headlines

REVELATION 8

We live between the times of the divinely-sent historical plagues of Egypt and the divinely-sent future plagues of the end of the age. Because of the instant access the news media provides to world events, we are well aware of the kinds of plagues that the world has endured during the past several decades. Rivers overflow and kill many. Hurricanes and tornadoes kill. The scourge of AIDS devastates some Third-World countries and snuffs out thousands of lives in North America.

Christian people are right to view many such disasters as the natural consequences of living in a fallen universe. We are right to say that God has permitted them, though we cannot say that He has directly caused them (unlike the Egyptian plagues). But how are we to respond when plagues hit us personally or the people we know and love?

First, we can acknowledge that God is just as sovereign in the evil He permits as He is in His direct acts of judgment. When people are killed in natural disasters, we can be certain that the situation did not surprise God. It may seem tragic, even senseless in our eyes, but He has permitted this to happen…for a purpose known only to Him.

Second, we can pray that God's people who live through disasters will be victorious in holding on to God by faith.

Finally, and perhaps most urgent of all, we can see natural disasters as occasions in which people are brought face-to-face with eternal issues. People often hear the gospel more clearly in the face of nature's plagues, and God lovingly uses us in these life-and-death moments to reach people at a level we may rarely touch at any other time or in any other way.

Horatio Spafford's testimony, written more than a century ago in the face of personal loss and disaster, has reached thousands of people with the hope of the gospel. After his children were lost at sea, he penned these powerful words:

When peace, like a river, attendeth my way,
When sorrows like sea billows roll;
Whatever my lot, thou hast taught me to say,
"It is well, it is well with my soul."
Though Satan should buffet, though trials should come,
Let this blest assurance control,
That Christ has regarded my helpless estate,
And hath shed his own blood for my soul.

Prayer

Lord God, help me to trust in Your loving care, both when my circumstances are good and when plagues seem overwhelming. Help me, like the songwriter, to confess, "It is well with my soul."

Revelation

Chapter 8

Preview

Now it really gets ugly, as the stormy season of end-time tribulation begins pouring down with a vengeance.

When He opened the seventh seal, there was **silence in heaven** for about half an hour. **2** Then I saw the seven angels who stand in the presence of God; **seven trumpets** were given to them. **3** Another angel, with a gold incense burner, came and stood at the altar. He was given a large amount of incense to offer with the prayers of all the saints on the gold altar in front of the throne. **4** The smoke of the incense, with the prayers of the saints, went up in the presence of God from the angel's hand. **5** The angel took the incense burner, filled it with fire from the altar, and hurled it to the earth; there were thunders, rumblings, lightnings, and an earthquake. **6** And the seven angels who had the seven trumpets prepared to blow them.

7 The first angel blew his trumpet, and hail and fire, mixed with blood, were **hurled to the earth**. So a third of the earth was burned up, a third of the trees were burned up, and all the green grass was **burned up**.

8 The second angel blew his trumpet, and something like a great mountain ablaze with fire was hurled into the sea. So a third of the sea became blood, **9** a third of the living creatures in

Living Insights

"silence in heaven"
Heaven is quiet for the first time in the whole book. But this is merely the calm before the storm.

"seven trumpets"
The scroll has now been opened to reveal seven destructive judgments. Others (the bowl judgments) will follow in chapter 16.

"hurled to the earth"
The season of intercession thunders to a close as the censer which once held the prayers of the saints is flung to the ground.

"burned up"
The same God who spoke the world into being now "uncreates" it one piece at a time by His command.

"Wormwood"
Wormwood is an extremely bitter yet not poisonous plant, made famous as the name of the junior demon in C.S. Lewis' *Screwtape Letters*.

"without light"
God had promised Noah that day and night would endlessly repeat as long as there was an earth. At this point, the earth is ceasing to exist.

Word Study

"live"

The Greek verb *katoikeo* [kah toi KEH oh] is a compound of two words: the preposition *kata*, meaning *down*, and the verb *oikeo*, meaning *to house* or *to live in a house*. In Revelation *katoikeo* is always used in a negative sense to describe the inhabitants of the earth who have become antagonistic to God. The phrase "those who live on the earth" (or something similar) occurs twelve of the thirteen times *katoikeo* is used in Revelation (3:10; 6:10; 8:13; 11:10; 13:8,12,14; 17:2,8).

the sea died, and a third of the ships were destroyed.

10 The third angel blew his trumpet, and a great star, blazing like a torch, fell from heaven. It fell on a third of the rivers and springs of water. **11** The name of the star is **Wormwood**, and a third of the waters became wormwood. So, many of the people died from the waters, because they had been made bitter.

12 The fourth angel blew his trumpet, and a third of the sun was struck, a third of the moon, and a third of the stars, so that a third of them were darkened. A third of the day was **without light**, and the night as well.

13 I looked, and I heard an eagle, flying in mid-heaven, saying in a loud voice, "Woe! Woe! Woe to those who **live** on the earth, because of the remaining trumpet blasts that the three angels are about to sound!"

End-Times Insight

Do you fully realize the peril your unsaved friends are in? Enough to warn them?

Tempting the Rattlesnake

REVELATION 9

An episode of the television western *Gunsmoke* once featured a huckster who traveled from town to town with a huge rattlesnake in a glass cage. He collected bets that no one could place his hand against the glass and keep it there when the rattlesnake struck.

The gullible townspeople bet on their fellow citizen who volunteered his courage. After all bets were collected, the huckster tore the cover off the glass cage, revealing a huge reptile coiling and buzzing his rattles. The man moved his hand toward the glass and the snake coiled even tighter. As soon as the hand touched the glass, the snake struck with fury. Involuntarily the man jerked his hand away. The huckster collected his money from the bets and left for the next town. He knew the glass would hold. There was nothing to fear but fear itself. He played on that fear to earn a living.

That story is a great picture of spiritual warfare. The snake is the devil and the forces of evil. The glass is Jesus. As long as we stay on the right side of the glass, we have nothing to fear. Real danger lurks on the wrong side of the glass, but we are safe no matter how fearful things appear (from Max Anders, *Spiritual Warfare*).

Keeping a balanced understanding of the real but limited power of supernatural evil is a challenge. C. S. Lewis wrote in *The Screwtape Letters,* "There are two equal and opposite errors into which our race can fall about the devils. One is to disbelieve in their existence. The other is to believe and to feel an excessive and unhealthy interest in them. They themselves are equally pleased by both errors, and hail a materialist or a magician with the same delight."

We may place too much emphasis on the demonic, claiming that "the devil made me do it." Or we may see demons behind every painful situation in life. The witness of Revelation 9 is that demons are real and powerful. Yet Jesus is also real. And more powerful.

All this talk about devils and demons may tempt some of us to ignore the demonic altogether, to believe that what we can't see can't hurt us. But the Bible teaches us that we are in a battle, that we must stay on constant alert against the reality of demonic influence (1Pt 5:8), that we must put on our spiritual armor—a metaphor for living in faith and obedience to Christ. Ephesians 6:11 says, "Put on the full armor of God so that you can stand against the tactics of the Devil," while James 4:7 delivers the instruction to "stand up to the Devil and he will flee from you."

Alertness. Armor. Resistance.

These are the keys to effective spiritual warfare.

Prayer

Lord God, I claim Your promise of protection from the direct onslaughts of evil spirits, today and every day. Thank You, God, for Your heavenly protection.

Chapter 9

Up to now, human beings have only been harmed indirectly by the fury of the trumpet judgments. The next ones, though, are a direct hit.

The fifth angel blew his trumpet, and I saw a **star that had fallen** from heaven to earth. The key to the shaft of the abyss was given to him. 2 He opened the shaft of the abyss, and smoke came up out of the shaft like smoke from a great furnace so that the sun and the air were darkened by the smoke from the shaft. 3 Then out of the smoke locusts came to the earth, and power was given to them like the power that scorpions have on the earth. 4 They were told not to harm the grass of the earth, or any green plant, or any tree, but **only people** who do not have God's seal on their foreheads. 5 They were not permitted to kill them, but were to torment them for five months; their torment is like the torment caused by a scorpion when it strikes a man. 6 In those days people will seek death and will not find it; they will long to die, but death will flee from them.

7 The appearance of the locusts was like horses equipped for battle. On their heads were something like gold crowns; their faces were like men's faces; 8 they had hair like women's hair; their teeth were like lions' teeth; 9 they had chests like iron breastplates; the sound of their wings was like the sound of char-

Living Insights

"star that had fallen"
Probably an angel. And you'll see the same one with the same key again in chapter 20, only this time to lock the abyss back again.

"only people"
These devouring demons are so powerful, they can hone in on humans and leave the grass under their feet untouched.

"angel of the abyss"
For the first (but not the last) time in Revelation, the word *angel* is applied to evil supernatural beings.

"Euphrates"
This river marked Israel's OT border and the remote edge of the Roman empire. When an advancing army reached this far, it meant trouble.

"two hundred million"
This is the largest precise number found in the New Testament. No human army has ever reached this size.

"did not repent"
Nothing is more tragic than a person so hardened by sin, that even when staring death in the face, he refuses God's grace.

Word Study

"a b y s s"

The Greek noun *abus-sos* [AH booss ahss] comes from the word *bussos* (also spelled *buthos*), meaning *depth* or *bottom*, and the letter *alpha* that negates it. Thus, *abussos* refers to something with no depth or bottom, a bottomless hole or pit. In Revelation *abussos* has three connotations. It refers to the present prison-like realm of certain classes of demons (9:1-2,11), the place of the beast's origin (11:7; 17:8), and the place of Satan's imprisonment during the millennium (20:1,3).

iots with many horses rushing into battle; **10** and they had tails with stingers, like scorpions, so that with their tails they had the power to harm people for five months. **11** They had as their king the **angel of the abyss**; his name in Hebrew is Abaddon, and in Greek he has the name Apollyon. **12** The first woe has passed. There are still two more woes to come after this.

13 The sixth angel blew his trumpet. From the four horns of the gold altar that is before God, I heard a voice **14** say to the sixth angel who had the trumpet, "Release the four angels bound at the great river **Euphrates**." **15** So the four angels who were prepared for the hour, day, month, and year were released to kill a third of the human race. **16** The number of mounted troops was **two hundred million**; I heard their number. **17** This is how I saw the horses in my vision: the horsemen had breastplates that were fiery red, hyacinth blue, and sulfur yellow. The heads of the horses were like lions' heads, and from their mouths came fire, smoke, and sulfur. **18** A third of the human race was killed by these three plagues—by the fire, the smoke, and the sulfur that came from their mouths. **19** For the power of the horses is in their mouths and in their tails, because their tails, like snakes, have heads, and they inflict injury with them.

20 The rest of the people, who were not killed by these plagues, **did not repent** of the works of their hands to stop worshiping demons and idols of gold, silver, bronze, stone, and wood, which are not able to see, hear, or walk. **21** And they did not repent of their murders, their sorceries, their sexual immorality, or their thefts.

End-Times Insight

Yes, there are demons at work in this world,
but in Christ, you have nothing to fear.

The Bitter with the Sweet

REVELATION 10

Mike and Trina are the loving parents of Chris, a high-school senior, and Casey, a twelve-year-old. Casey was born with a severe case of cerebral palsy which has left her mentally retarded and confined to a wheelchair. She is a blessing to many who meet her. She smiles and gurgles with pleasure when people give her attention. And as her mother, who is a neonatal-care nurse, has told me, "Because of Casey, I've been able to counsel many parents who have just learned that their newborn is mentally or physically handicapped. I've been able to witness to Christ's love and grace in ways that would never have been possible without Casey. When God sent us Casey, he entrusted us with a precious treasure."

But Casey is also a great burden. She will never walk. Mealtime is difficult. Frankly, her distorted features are hard to look at. She requires her own special caregiver when Mike and Trina are away from home. And one can only imagine the strain this kind of unending responsibility places on their marriage. Many, in fact, do not survive the stress that a handicapped child brings. When I once complimented Mike for the way he has cheerfully accepted responsibility for Casey, he replied, "I didn't think I had a choice. There really wasn't an option."

They know firsthand the way John must have felt in Revelation 10.

Today we are not in the same situation that John was in when he received the Word of God directly. Yet all who know Christ and his Word should expect that Word to be both sweet and sour. Yes, wonderful sweetness comes from realizing that God has given us His marvelous Word. Yes, great delight results from meditating on the truths of Scripture. Thank God for the "sweet as honey in my mouth" aspect of knowing the Word of God.

Sometimes, though, by God's design, that Word becomes a burden. When we share the gospel with people and they refuse to believe in Christ, we experience the bitterness of the Word. When we come to understand that God permits His own people to be tested and tried, we understand the sour aspect of the Word. When we recognize that God's Word tells us He plans for many of His people to be martyred for the sake of Christ, and for even more of His people to experience great tribulation, we can identify with John's words, "My stomach became bitter."

One challenge we face from this chapter of Scripture is to accept both the sour with the sweet, the bitter with the pleasant, the sorrowful with the joyful. Only when we embrace both aspects of the impact that the Word of God makes will we be completely true to his Word.

Prayer

Father, help me realize that Your Word may impact my life in ways both sweet and bitter. And help me be courageous enough to share Your Word with others, both when it soothes and when it hurts.

Chapter 10

Preview

At the height of the trumpet judgments, another interlude suspends the drama, but not the certainty, of God's plan.

Then I saw another mighty angel coming down from heaven, surrounded by a cloud, with a rainbow over his head. His face was like the sun, his legs were like fiery pillars, **2** and he had a **little scroll** opened in his hand. He put his right foot on the sea, his left on the land, **3** and he cried out with a loud voice like a roaring lion. When he cried out, the **seven thunders** spoke with their voices. **4** And when the seven thunders spoke, I was about to write. Then I heard a **voice** from heaven, saying, "Seal up what the seven thunders said, and **do not write** it down!"

5 Then the angel that I had seen standing on the sea and on the land raised his right hand to heaven. **6** He swore an oath by the One who lives **forever and ever**, who created heaven and what is in it, the earth and what is in it, and the sea and what is in it: "There will no longer be an **interval of time**, **7** but in the days of the sound of the seventh angel, when he will blow his trumpet, then God's hidden plan will be completed, as He announced to His servants the prophets."

8 Now the voice that I heard from heaven spoke to me again and said, "Go, take the scroll that lies open in the hand of the angel who is standing on the sea and on the land."

Living Insights

"little scroll"
This is not the sealed scroll from chapter 5, but a special message to John concerning the churches.

"seven thunders"
This is the only appearance of these mysterious speakers in Scripture. Whoever they are, they must be awesome.

"do not write"
The Bible doesn't reveal every detail of the end-time judgments. But you can be sure it gives us all we need to know.

"forever and ever"
Imagine the new relevance this phrase would have in light of the now obvious vulnerability of the earth.

"interval of time"
These unknown lengths of time make end-times date-setting a waste. But the day is coming when everything will happen bang-bang-bang.

"take and eat it"
John, a mere mortal, has access to this heavenly scroll—as do all of us who bear God's message of salvation and judgment.

Word Study

"voice"

The Greek noun *phone* [foh NAY] normally refers to the sound of ordinary speech, but it can also refer to other sounds made by the mouth or to noises in general. The most common meaning of *phone* is *voice* or the *sound of a voice* (10:3-4,7-8), but it also has other uses, such as the notes of musical instruments (8:13; 18:22). Sometimes in Revelation, *phone* refers to the rumblings of thunder that signify the presence and power of God (4:5; 8:5; 11:19; 14:2; 16:18; 19:6).

9 So I went to the angel and asked him to give me the little scroll. He said to me, "**Take and eat it**; it will be bitter in your stomach, but it will be as sweet as honey in your mouth."

10 Then I took the little scroll from the angel's hand and ate it. It was as sweet as honey in my mouth, but when I ate it, my stomach became bitter. **11** And I was told, "You must prophesy again about many peoples, nations, languages, and kings."

End-Times Insight

God's Word will prove itself true
no matter how anybody feels about it.

When Truth Takes Action

The World Wide Web and the Internet zoomed from "what's that?" to universal awareness among North Americans during the 1990s. Even people without computer savvy quickly became part of the "dot.com" generation. The Web became a seemingly universal tool in people's lives, giving them confidence that virtually every fact and factoid in the universe could be accessed with just a few computer clicks.

The Internet, however, has not helped people discern truth. Every lie, rumor, and false claim you can imagine has come via "www." Moral filth has poured from thousands of web sites. While millions have cheered the awesome power now available to them, alarmed voices continue to point to both the factual errors and the moral bankruptcy purveyed through the 'Net.

The Internet vividly illustrates what happens when awesome power is neutral about truth and morality. It makes a lot of noise and attracts a lot of attention. But at what cost—to itself and its culture? Too often, however, contemporary Christianity has painted just the opposite picture: truth without any power at all. This chapter of Revelation prods us to see that God intends His truth to be proclaimed with power.

Our world thinks the Internet is so great. When Christianity arrived two thousand years ago, entrusted into the hearts of only a few followers of Jesus, who would have guessed it had the power to sweep over an unknown world and change the course of history for more than two thousand years? Perhaps even now we stand on the verge of new and powerful manifestations of the truth of the gospel that will impact the world in ways that make the Internet look like a passing fad.

Need we wait until then to see the powerful truth of God proclaimed in a world that sometimes questions whether there is any such thing as truth? The gospel is a word from God. It is enabled by the Spirit of God. When His people proclaim it, no one can stop it without divine permission.

We are to stand firm. Firm that the Word of God is truth for a world that has denied truth. Firm that God has all the power in the universe to see to it that His truth will be powerfully manifested. Firm that God intends His church to be an agent of His truth and His power.

The world has seen power without truth and is impressed. The world has seen truth without power and has ignored it. But what would this world do if truth were to be coupled with unmistakable divine power? The world is waiting—in fact, dying—to see it.

Prayer

Lord God of Moses and Elijah, raise up the prophets of fire for our day. If You want to call me to such a task, here am I, send me. I will willingly pay the price.

Chapter 11

Preview

John describes the final days, just before the last trumpet shouts that time is at an end.

Then I was given a measuring reed like a rod, with these words: "Go and measure God's sanctuary and the altar, and count those who worship there. **2** But exclude the courtyard outside the sanctuary. Don't measure it, because it is given to the nations, and they will trample the holy city for **forty-two months**. **3** I will empower my two witnesses, and they will prophesy for 1,260 days, dressed in sackcloth." **4** These are the two olive trees and the **two lampstands** that stand before the Lord of the earth. **5** If anyone wants to harm them, fire comes from their mouths and consumes their enemies; if anyone wants to harm them, he must be killed in this way. **6** These men have the power to close the sky so that it does not rain during the days of their prophecy. They also have power over the waters to turn them into blood, and to strike the earth with any plague whenever they want.

7 When they finish their testimony, the **beast** that comes up out of the abyss will make war with them, conquer them, and kill them. **8** Their dead bodies will lie in the public square of the great city, which is called, prophetically, **Sodom and Egypt**, where also their Lord was crucified. **9** And representatives from the peoples, tribes, languages, and nations will view their bodies for **three and a half days** and not permit their bodies to be put into a tomb. **10** Those who live on the earth will gloat over them and celebrate and send gifts to one another, because these two prophets tormented those who live on the earth.

11 But after the three and a half days, the breath of life from God entered them, and they stood on their feet. So great fear fell on those who saw them. **12** Then they heard a loud voice from heaven saying to them, "Come up here." They went up to heaven in a cloud, while their enemies watched them. **13** At that moment a violent earthquake took place, a tenth of the city fell, and seven thousand people were killed in the earthquake. The survivors

Word Study
"beast"

The Greek noun *therion* [thay REE ahn] means *beast, creature,* or *animal*. However, Revelation uses it in reference to real animals only twice (6:8; 18:2). In all other uses, *therion* is a vivid personification of either the evil leader of a Satan-led empire (11:17; 13:1-18; 17:3-17; 19:19) or his henchman, the false prophet (13:11-17; 16:13). Revelation 19:20 indicates that *therion* can refer to an individual person since the beast and the false prophet are cast into the lake of fire.

were terrified and gave **glory to** the **God** of heaven. **14** The second woe has passed. Take note: the third woe is coming quickly!

15 The seventh angel blew his trumpet, and there were loud voices in heaven saying:

> The kingdom of the world has become
> the kingdom
> of our Lord and of His Messiah,
> and He will reign forever and ever!

16 The twenty-four elders, who were seated before God on their thrones, fell on their faces and worshiped God, **17** saying:

> We thank You, Lord God, the Almighty,
> who is and who was,
> because You have taken Your great power
> and have begun to reign.
> **18** The nations were angry, but Your wrath
> has come.
> The time has come for the dead to be
> judged,
> and to give the reward to Your servants
> the prophets,

Living Insights

"forty-two months"
Equals the 1,260 days in the next verse, and stands for a limited time of intense suffering.

"two lampstands"
This imagery used for the seven churches in chapter 1 might mean that the two witnesses represent churches.

"Sodom and Egypt"
Sodom—the prototype of the sinful, pleasure-seeking city. And Egypt—where God's people had been enslaved.

"three and a half days"
The witnesses' ministry lasted 3 1/2 years, their deaths 3 1/2 days—the numerical symbol for incompletion, or half of seven.

"glory to God"
The right words, but the wrong heart—a person admitting the obvious through clenched teeth, red eyes, and a raised fist.

"ark of His covenant"
It had been lost to history six centuries before Christ. Here in heavenly form stands the unshakable proof of God's unbreakable promises.

to the saints, and to those who fear Your name,
    both small and great,
and the time has come to destroy those who
    destroy the earth.

19 God's sanctuary in heaven was opened, and the **ark of His covenant** appeared in His sanctuary. There were lightnings, rumblings, thunders, an earthquake, and severe hail.

End-Times Insight

*The people of God exist in all times
to speak God's Word at all costs.*

Piercing the Darkness

REVELATION 12

A merican Christian novelist Frank Peretti created a sensation among many evangelical believers during the late 1980s. Both *This Present Darkness* (1986) and *Piercing the Darkness* (1989) portrayed the comings and goings of fictional Christian heroes. Their deeds were described largely as the outcome of invisible, ongoing spiritual warfare between angels and demons on planet Earth. Peretti's strongest point in writing was to emphasize passionately that angels and demons are real personal beings that influence earthly events. His loving descriptions of the angels made me long to meet them. As he told of demons, I shuddered at the stench of hell attached to these batlike creatures.

I remember well the discussions I had with my students when Peretti's works first came out. Had he gone too far in trying to make the invisible world visible? Was his theology of spiritual warfare truly biblical? Are angels really that powerful? Does the spiritual world really work the way it does in Peretti's fiction? We finally concluded that ultimately, whether things are exactly as Peretti portrayed them or not, he had forced us to come face-to-face with truths that we believed in but seldom thought about: angels are real spiritual beings that serve God, and demons are real spiritual beings that serve evil. Both are active in the affairs of earth. There is more to the war between good and evil than meets the eye.

Revelation 12 functions in a similar way. It begins a great sky-drama that serves as an epic intermission between the terror of the trumpets and the further judgments to come. It portrays a real, personal devil who hates God and will do anything he can to make war against God's people. But guess what? The people of God are just as real as the devil is. God sees and knows them and promises His protection as they struggle against the devil. The ultimate hero of the drama is Jesus, who will rule the nations with an iron scepter.

Even in our present visible world, the most real thing about our existence is the age-long struggle of God's people versus the devil. And throughout human history, the way God's people have pierced the darkness is through keeping God's commands and holding to a firm testimony (v. 17).

As a believer in Christ, pierce your own darkness by remembering that your obedience to God counts. Take this as an opportunity to evaluate whether you're holding to His teachings. Commit yourself to dealing with the specific areas in your life where your obedience could be more complete. Ask God to show you how to cling more firmly to Jesus—and to bear witness to others that he is the true Ruler of the universe.

Prayer

Lord, help me conquer the devil through keeping Your commands and holding to a firm testimony. I pray this because of my faith in the powerful blood of the Lamb, which makes my victory secure.

Chapter 12

Preview

Sit back for the opening act of a two-part drama, the story of a great spiritual conflict with eternal consequences.

A great sign appeared in heaven: a woman **clothed with the sun**, with the moon under her feet, and a crown of twelve **stars** on her head. ² She was pregnant and cried out in labor and agony to give birth. ³ Then another sign appeared in heaven: There was a great fiery red dragon having seven heads and ten horns, and on his heads were seven diadems. ⁴ His tail swept away a third of the stars in heaven and hurled them to the earth. And the dragon stood in front of the woman who was about to give birth, so that when she did give birth he might **devour her child**. ⁵ But she gave birth to a Son—a male who is going to shepherd all nations with an iron scepter—and her child was caught up to God and to His throne. ⁶ The woman fled into the wilderness, where she had a place prepared by God, to be fed there for 1,260 days.

⁷ Then war broke out in heaven: **Michael** and his angels fought against the dragon. The dragon and his angels also fought, ⁸ but he could not prevail, and there was no place for them in heaven any longer. ⁹ So the great dragon was thrown out—the ancient serpent, who is called the **Devil and Satan**, the one who deceives the whole world. He was thrown to earth, and his angels with him.

Living Insights

"clothed with the sun"
This is the way God sees his people—as glorious as the sun, as beautiful as a night spent under the stars.

"devour her child"
Satan's animosity foretold in Genesis 3:15 extends from the Garden of Eden to the lake of fire. Remember him trying to kill all the baby boys in Bethlehem?

"Michael"
The other Bible texts (from Daniel and Jude) that mention him by name confirm his role as a warrior angel.

"Devil and Satan"
Devil is the Greek word for *slanderer*. Satan is a Hebrew word meaning *adversary*. He is both at the same time.

"wilderness"
God, in His sovereignty, allows the devil to go so far and no further. He has ways to shield us from Satan's fury.

"opened its mouth"
God will do whatever He wants to protect His people, even if it means bringing the forces of nature to their aid.

10 Then I heard a loud voice in heaven say:

> The salvation and the power and the
>   kingdom of our God
> and the authority of His Messiah
>   have now come,
> because the accuser of our brothers has
>   been thrown out:
> the one who accuses them before our
>   God day and night.

11 They conquered him by the blood
>   of the Lamb
> and by the word of their testimony,
> for they did not love their lives in the
>   face of death.

12 Therefore rejoice, O heavens, and you
>   who dwell in them!
> Woe to the earth and the sea,
> for the Devil has come down to you
>   with great fury,
> because he knows he has a short time.

13 When the dragon saw that he had been thrown to earth, he persecuted the woman who gave birth to the male. **14** The woman was given two wings of a great eagle, so that she could fly from the serpent's presence to her place in the **wilderness**, where she was fed for a time, times, and half a time. **15** From his mouth the serpent spewed water like a river after the woman, to sweep her away in a torrent. **16** But the earth helped the woman: the earth **opened its mouth** and swallowed up the river that the dragon had spewed from his mouth. **17** So the dragon was furious with the woman and left to wage war against the rest of her offspring—those who keep the commandments of God and have the testimony about Jesus. **18** He stood on the sand of the sea.

Word Study

"s t a r"

The Greek noun *aster* [ah STAIR] is used figuratively in Revelation to speak of several powerful persons, both good and evil. Jesus is "the Bright Morning Star" (22:16) and the "seven stars" in His hand are angels (1:16,20; 2:1; 3:1). Satan leads "a third of the stars in heaven" (12:4), probably angels who rebelled against God. He or one of his demons is the "star...from heaven" that opens the abyss (9:1-2). The "twelve stars" on the woman's crown refer to the tribes of Israel (12:1-20; see Genesis 37:9–10).

End-Times Insight

Pray for God's people like there's no tomorrow, because the devil is preying too.

detail from

The Resurrection of the Dead

LUCA SIGNORELLI (1441-1523)

Scala/Art Resource, NY

Then I heard something like the voice of a vast multitude,
like the sound of cascading waters, and like the rumbling
of loud thunder, saying: "Hallelujah – because our Lord
God, the Almighty, has begun to reign! Let us be glad,
rejoice, and give Him glory, because the marriage of the
Lamb has come, and His wife has prepared herself."

REVELATION 19:6-7

from The Altarpiece of St. John Baptist and St. John Evangelist

Apocalyptic Vision of St. John Evangelist

HANS MEMLING (1433-1494)

Erich Lessing/Art Resource, NY

I, John, your brother and partner in the tribulation, kingdom, and perseverance in Jesus, was on the island called Patmos because of God's word and the testimony about Jesus. I was in the Spirit on the Lord's day, and I heard behind me a loud voice like a trumpet saying, "Write on a scroll what you see and send it to the seven churches."

REVELATION 1:9-11A

detail from The Ghent Altarpiece

The Adoration of the Lamb

JAN VAN EYCK (c.1390-1441)

Scala/Art Resource, NY

Then I looked, and heard the voice of many angels around the throne, and also of the living creatures, and of the elders. Their number was countless thousands, plus thousands of thousands. They said with a loud voice: "The Lamb who was slaughtered is worthy to receive power and riches and wisdom and strength and honor and glory and blessing!"

REVELATION 5:11-12

Four Horsemen of the Apocalypse
EDWARD JAKOB VON STEINLE (1810-1886)
Kunsthalle, Mannheim, Germany/SuperStock

I looked, and there was a white horse. The horseman on
it had a bow; a crown was given to him, and he went out
as a victor to conquer....Then another horse went out, a
fiery red one, and its horseman was empowered to take
peace from the earth....And I looked, and there was a
black horse. The horseman on it had a balance scale in
his hand.

REVELATION 6:2,4A,5B

Death on the Pale Horse

BENJAMIN WEST (1738-1820)

Pennsylvania Academy of the Fine Arts, Philadelphia

When He opened the fourth seal, I heard the voice of the fourth living creature say, "Come!" And I looked, and there was a pale green horse. The horseman on it was named Death, and Hades was following after him. Authority was given to them over a fourth of the earth, to kill by the sword, by famine, by plague, and by the wild animals of the earth.

REVELATION 6:7-8

St. Michael Slaying the Dragon
RAPHAEL (1483-1520)
Erich Lessing/Art Resource, NY

Michael and his angels fought against the dragon. The dragon and his angels also fought, but he could not prevail, and there was no place for them in heaven any longer. So the great dragon was thrown out – the ancient serpent, who is called the Devil and Satan, the one who deceives the whole world. He was thrown to earth, and his angels with him.

REVELATION 12:7B-9

The Number of the Beast Is 666

WILLIAM BLAKE (1757-1827)

Rosenbach Museum and Library, Philadelphia

And I saw a beast coming up out of the sea. He had ten
horns and seven heads. On his horns were ten diadems,
and on his heads were blasphemous names. The beast I
saw was like a leopard, his feet were like a bear's, and his
mouth was like a lion's mouth. The dragon gave him his
power, his throne, and great authority....His number is 666.

REVELATION 13:1-2,18B

detail from
Acts of the Antichrist
LUCA SIGNORELLI (1441-1523)
Scala/Art Resource, NY

A mouth was given to him to speak boasts and blasphemies. He was also given authority to act for forty-two months. He began to speak blasphemies against God: to blaspheme His name and His dwelling – those who dwell in heaven. And he was permitted to wage war against the saints and to conquer them.

REVELATION 13:5-7A

The Great Day of His Wrath

JOHN MARTIN (1789-1854)

Tate Gallery, London/Art Resource, NY

The first angel blew his trumpet, and hail and fire, mixed with blood, were hurled to the earth. So a third of the earth was burned up, a third of the trees were burned up, and all the green grass was burned up. The second angel blew his trumpet, and something like a great mountain ablaze with fire was hurled into the sea. So a third of the sea became blood.

REVELATION 8:7-8

The Destruction of the Beast and the False Prophet

BENJAMIN WEST (1738-1820)

The Minneapolis Institute of Arts

But the beast was taken prisoner, and along with him the false prophet, who had performed signs on his authority, by which he deceived those who accepted the mark of the beast and those who worshiped his image. Both of them were thrown alive into the lake of fire that burns with sulfur.

REVELATION 19:20

The Angel Michael Binding Satan

He Cast Him into the Bottomless Pit and Shut Him Up

WILLIAM BLAKE (1757-1827)

Fogg Art Museum, Harvard University Art Museums, Gift of W. A. White

Then I saw an angel coming down from heaven with the key to the abyss and a great chain in his hand. He seized the dragon, that ancient serpent who is the Devil and Satan, and bound him for a thousand years. He threw him into the abyss, closed it, and put a seal on it so that he would no longer deceive the nations until the thousand years were completed.

REVELATION 20:1-3A

The Resurrection of the Dead

PAUL CHENAVARD (1807-1895)

Erich Lessing/Art Resource, NY

I also saw the souls of those who had been beheaded because of their testimony about Jesus and because of God's word, who had not worshiped the beast or his image, and who had not accepted the mark on their foreheads or their hands. They came to life and reigned with the Messiah for a thousand years.

REVELATION 20:4B

The Last Judgment

PETER VON CORNELIUS (1783-1867)

Erich Lessing/Art Resource, NY

Then I saw a great white throne and One seated on it.
Earth and heaven fled from His presence, and no place
was found for them. I also saw the dead, the great and the
small, standing before the throne, and books were
opened. Another book was opened, which is the book of
life, and the dead were judged according to their works
by what was written in the books.

REVELATION 20:11-12

The Last Judgment

JEAN COUSIN THE YOUNGER (1522-1594)

Musee du Louvre, Paris/Superstock

Then the sea gave up its dead, and Death and Hades gave
up their dead; all were judged according to their works.
Death and Hades were thrown into the lake of fire. This is
the second death, the lake of fire. And anyone not found
written in the book of life was thrown into the lake of fire.

REVELATION 20:13-15

The Plains of Heaven

JOHN MARTIN (1789-1854)

Tate Gallery, London/Art Resource, NY

Then he showed me the river of living water, sparkling
like crystal, flowing from the throne of God and of the
Lamb down the middle of the broad street of the city. On
both sides of the river was the tree of life bearing twelve
kinds of fruit, producing its fruit every month. The leaves
of the tree are for healing the nations.

REVELATION 22:1-2

from The Last Judgment
Christ in Majesty

CEILING FRESCO, VORAU, AUSTRIA (1716)

Erich Lessing/Art Resource, NY

The city does not need the sun or the moon to shine on it, because God's glory illuminates it, and its lamp is the Lamb. The nations will walk in its light, and the kings of the earth will bring their glory into it. Each day its gates will never close because it will never be night there. They will bring the glory and honor of the nations into it.

REVELATION 21:23-26

Avoiding the Mark of the Beast

REVELATION 13

One of the most remarkable tours available to visitors to Washington, D.C., is the Bureau of Engraving and Printing. My family was fascinated to learn about the process by which paper money is manufactured. One great task of the government is to make counterfeiting difficult. Many agents of the Treasury Department spend their entire careers tracking down fake money. A member of our group asked the tour guide, "What's the best way to avoid receiving counterfeit bills?" The answer was simple but profound: "Just learn the marks of a true bill. Then you won't have any trouble spotting the fake ones."

That guideline holds true for chapter 13 of Revelation. It's all about a counterfeit Jesus, an Antichrist. In discussions I have had with sincere Christian people, they have mentioned that they are afraid they will one day unwittingly receive "the mark of the beast." Some have avoided receiving U.S. Social Security numbers. Others have argued that body tattoos are, for this reason, evil. Still others have tried to figure out what the mark might literally be so they can avoid ever receiving it.

This whole exercise misses the point. In Revelation, those who are redeemed, those whose names are in the Book of Life, those who have already received the seal of God which marks them as His people, have no worries about being stamped with the mark of the beast. Because they have a true relationship with Jesus—the true Christ—they are never in danger of being duped by the pretending christ of Satan. Their close fellowship with Jesus makes them "antichrist proof."

Whether we are the generation who will see the coming of the final Antichrist is ultimately in God's hands—and frankly, none of our business. We should be concerned instead about the many antichrists who are already working—those who already use political, religious, or economic pressure to pull us from loyalty to Jesus Christ. This was the warning John made in his First Epistle: "Children, it is the last hour. And just as you have heard that the Antichrist is coming, so now many antichrists have appeared. By this we know that it is the last hour" (1 John 2:18).

So how can you avoid being marked by the beast of our days? The answer is simple: Maintain a close personal relationship with Jesus, and you will never be deceived by those who are cheap imitations of him.

Prayer

Lord, I acknowledge that when I am left to myself, I can be easily deceived by the devil. Help me commit myself to a close personal commitment with You so that I can always recognize his ways.

Chapter 13

Preview

This grand drama of the ages now becomes a full-scale horror story, featuring the ultimate monsters of power and corruption.

And I saw a **beast** coming up out of the sea. He had ten horns and seven heads. On his horns were ten diadems, and on his heads were blasphemous names. 2 The beast I saw was like a leopard, his feet were like a bear's, and his mouth was like a lion's mouth. The dragon gave him his power, his throne, and great authority. 3 One of his heads appeared to be **fatally wounded**, but his fatal wound was healed. The whole earth was amazed and followed the beast. 4 They worshiped the dragon because he gave authority to the beast. And they worshiped the beast, saying, "Who is like the beast? Who is able to wage war against him?"

5 A mouth was given to him to speak boasts and blasphemies. He was also given authority to act for **forty-two months**. 6 He began to speak blasphemies against God: to blaspheme His name and His dwelling—those who dwell in heaven. 7 And he was permitted to wage war against the saints and to conquer them. He was also given authority over every tribe, people, language, and nation. 8 All those who live on the earth will worship him, everyone whose name was not written from the **foundation of the world** in the book of life of the Lamb who was slaughtered.

Living Insights

"beast...another beast"
Meet Satan's henchmen—raw political power embodied in the Antichrist; religious deception embodied in the False Prophet.

"fatally wounded"
This is a counterfeit copy of the slaughtered lamb in 5:6, only this time an evil parody of the true Christ.

"forty-two months",
Continue to note the limits God places on this season of evil. If the devil were in charge, you can bet it would last a lot longer than that.

"foundation of the world"
Even in the midst of such frightening deception, God's plan pulls rank on these maniac masterminds.

"like a lamb"
Everything about these three—the Antichrist, the False Prophet, and the devil—is a mockery, a cheap imitation of the Trinity.

"spirit to the image"
Ventriloquists were already making idols talk in John's day. Imagine the techno-wizardry that will give this end-time image a virtual reality.

Word Study

"666"

Hebrew and Greek (among other languages) were used in the ancient practice of *gematria* to attach a numerical value to each letter of the alphabet. Therefore, the numerical value of a word (such as a person's name) could be determined by finding the sum of the numerical values of all its letters. Revelation specifically refers to "the number of his ['the beast's'] name" (13:17; 15:2), so the 666 in 13:18 simply provides a cryptic way of identifying the beast.

⁹ If anyone has an ear, he should listen:

¹⁰ If anyone is destined for captivity,
  into captivity he goes.
  If anyone is to be killed with a sword,
  with a sword he will be killed.

Here is the endurance and the faith of the saints.

¹¹ Then I saw **another beast** coming up out of the earth; he had two horns **like a lamb**, but he sounded like a dragon. ¹² He exercises all the authority of the first beast on his behalf and compels the earth and those who live on it to worship the first beast, whose fatal wound was healed. ¹³ He also performs great signs, even causing fire to come down from heaven to earth before people. ¹⁴ He deceives those who live on the earth because of the signs that he is permitted to perform on behalf of the beast, telling those who live on the earth to make an image of the beast who had the sword wound yet lived. ¹⁵ He was permitted to give a **spirit to the image** of the beast, so that the image of the beast could both speak and cause whoever would not worship the image of the beast to be killed. ¹⁶ And he requires everyone—small and great, rich and poor, free and slave—to be given a mark on his right hand or on his forehead, ¹⁷ so that no one can buy or sell unless he has the mark: the beast's name or the number of his name.

¹⁸ Here is wisdom: The one who has understanding must calculate the number of the beast, because it is the number of a man. His number is **666**.

End-Times Insight

You need discernment and you need it now.
You'll find it by spending lots of time with the real thing—Jesus.

The Final Cut

REVELATION 14

I grew up in Oklahoma, one of the great wheat-producing states in all of America. Nothing is more striking than the panorama of golden grain stretching as far as the eye can see. Even now, I can instantly call up the image of the grainfields being harvested by eight, ten, even a dozen combines all at once—work that would have taken hundreds of men to accomplish two centuries ago.

In chapter 14 of Revelation, all the world's people are classified as either grain or grapes. Grain is safely gathered; grapes are trodden in the winepress. Surely everyone who reads this chapter will want to be part of the harvest, not part of the vintage. The challenge is to live life now in order to be ready for harvest.

Imagine yourself as a stalk of grain. You would never have had life if the farmer had not planted you. You have gone through the proper life cycle, grown tall and produced mature kernels of wheat. Now all is ready. At last harvest day comes. You are gathered up into the landowner's barn. You have fulfilled the purpose of your existence.

So it is with our Christian life. We would never have had life if Christ had not purchased us. We show that we are God's people by living holy lives of obedience and purity. We are ready for the harvest day to come. Either by the death of our body or at the return of Christ, we will be gathered into His presence. This will truly fulfill our existence.

The nineteenth-century hymn writer Henry Alford expressed this so well in the song we usually sing only during the Thanksgiving season, "Come, Ye Thankful People, Come." Read again the words of the last stanza:

For the Lord our God shall come,
And shall take His harvest home;
From His field shall purge away
All that doth offend that day;
Give His angels charge at last
In the fire the tares to cast;
But the fruitful ears to store
In His garner evermore.

Prayer

Lord Jesus, thank You that all those You redeem will safely arrive in heaven. I commit to live my life now in holiness and purity. I long for the day when You will come and take Your harvest home.

Chapter 14

Preview

Part One of this titanic drama reaches its graphic conclusion, as all humanity finds itself divided into two very distinct camps.

Then I looked, and there on **Mount Zion** stood the Lamb, and with Him were 144,000 who had His name and His Father's name written on their foreheads. **2** I heard a sound from heaven like the sound of cascading waters and like the rumbling of loud thunder. The sound I heard was also like harpists playing on their harps. **3** They sang a new song before the throne and before the four living creatures and the elders, but no one could learn the song except the 144,000 who had been redeemed from the earth. **4** These are the ones not defiled with women, for they have kept their **virginity**. These are the ones who follow the Lamb wherever He goes. They were redeemed from the human race as firstfruits for God and the Lamb. **5** No lie was found in their mouths; they are blameless.

6 Then I saw another angel flying in mid-heaven, having the **eternal gospel** to announce to the inhabitants of the earth—to every nation, tribe, language, and people. **7** He spoke with a loud voice: "Fear God and give Him glory, because the hour of His judgment has come. **Worship the Maker** of heaven and earth, the sea and springs of water."

8 A second angel followed, saying: "It has fallen, Babylon the Great has fallen, who made all nations drink the wine of her sexual immorality, which brings wrath."

9 And a third angel followed them and spoke with a loud voice: "If anyone worships the beast and his image and receives a mark on his forehead or on his hand, **10** he will also drink the wine of God's wrath, which is mixed full strength in the cup of His anger. He will be tormented with fire and sulfur in the sight of the holy angels and in the sight of the Lamb, **11** and the smoke of their torment will go up forever and ever. There is **no rest** day or night for those who worship the beast and his image, or anyone who receives the mark of his name. **12** Here is the endurance

Word Study

" h e a v e n "

The Greek noun *oura-nos* [oo rah NAHSS] basically means *heaven* in both the Greek Old Testament (translating the Hebrew *shemayim*) and the New Testament. In Revelation, it is primarily seen as the celestial location of God's manifested presence, far above the earth (4:2). One special use of *ouranos* that appears in Revelation refers to heaven as the place of divine origin for certain things, such as angels and the New Jerusalem (3:12; 14:13; 18:1; 20:1; 21:2).

of the saints, who keep the commandments of God and the faith in Jesus."

13 Then I heard a voice from **heaven** saying, "Write: Blessed are the dead who die in the Lord from now on."

"Yes," says the Spirit, "let them rest from their labors, for their works follow them!"

14 Then I looked, and there was a white cloud, and One like the Son of Man was seated on the cloud, with a gold crown on His head and a sharp sickle in His hand. **15** Another angel came **out of the sanctuary**, crying out in a loud voice to the One who was seated on the cloud, "Use your sickle and reap, for the time to reap has come, since the harvest of the earth is ripe." **16** So the One seated on the cloud swung His sickle over the earth, and the earth was harvested.

17 Then another angel who also had a sharp sickle came out of the sanctuary in heaven. **18** Yet another angel, who had authority over fire, came from the altar, and he called with a loud voice to the one who had the sharp sickle, "Use your sharp sickle and gather the clusters of grapes from earth's vineyard, because its grapes have ripened." **19** So the angel swung his sickle toward earth and

Living Insights

"Mount Zion"
In contrast to the devil standing on "the sand of the sea" in 12:18, Jesus is planted on the immovable mountain of God.

"virginity"
More than sexual purity, this term stands for the spiritual purity of those who had stayed true to God.

"eternal gospel"
Their message is not the gospel of Christ's death and resurrection, but the good news (for believers) that the end has finally come.

"worship the Maker"
Even those who won't submit to God as Lord will someday find it hard to deny that He's at least the One in charge.

"no rest"
For the unrepentant, an eternity to regret their decision—pain without mercy, and not even death to relieve them.

"out of the sanctuary"
Jesus had said He did not know the day or hour of His return. Right here, the angel passes Him word from the Father. "OK, Son. It's time."

gathered the grapes from earth's vineyard, and he threw them into the great winepress of God's wrath. [20] Then the press was trampled outside the city, and blood flowed out of the press up to the horses' bridles for about one hundred eighty miles.

End-Times Insight

We are destined for an eternity spent in pure holiness. Start practicing it here and now.

The Song of the Lamb

REVELATION 15

My mother is one of the most Christlike persons I have ever known. A lifelong church member and faithful attender, she has for years faithfully sung all the songs in the well-loved hymnal from her fourth-pew seat. She, more than any other person, taught me the importance of joyful singing in worship. She taught me by her example that this is simply something that God's people do; they worship Him through singing.

Now, Mother's voice was never musically trained. Her alto singing is sometimes flat and tuneless. Nobody has ever asked her to join the choir. In fact, one of her favorite sayings is, "I must have a lot of music in me, because none of it has ever come out."

But Mother sings "The Song of the Lamb" very well. I don't mean with her physical lips, but from her heart. You see, lyrics and tune may change, but it is still the same song. Years may pass and circumstances may shift from joy to sorrow, but the song still resonates. People may laugh and the world may ignore it, but that's OK. The song isn't sung for them. It's performed for an audience of One, a heavenly throne with a worthy recipient.

If you have trouble singing "The Song of the Lamb," perhaps this old-fashioned excerpt from George Mueller, powerful Christian of an earlier generation will help:

"Are you able to say, from the acquaintance you have made with God, that He is a lovely Being? If not, let me affectionately entreat you to ask God to bring you to this, that you may admire His gentleness and kindness, that you may be able to say how good He is, and what a delight it is to the heart of God to do good to His children. Now the nearer we come to this in our inmost souls, the more ready we are to leave ourselves in His hands, satisfied with all His dealings with us. And when trial comes, we shall say: 'I will wait and see what good God will do to me by it, assured He will do it.' Thus we shall bear an honorable testimony before the world, and thus we shall strengthen the hands of others."

And thus we shall continue to sing, while God gives us breath.

Prayer

Lord, I long for the day that I will be in heaven with You. But I resolve not to wait till I get there to sing for You "The Song of the Lamb"—to grow as a singing worshiper in my life here and now.

Chapter 15

Preview

The curtain opens on the second act in this two-part drama, and those who are not ready for it are going to be bowled over.

Then I saw another great and awesome sign in heaven: seven angels with the seven last plagues, for with them, God's wrath will be completed. **2** I also saw something like a sea of glass mixed with fire, and those who had won the **victory** from the beast, his image, and the number of his name, were standing on the sea of glass with **harps from God**. **3** They sang the song of God's servant Moses, and the song of the Lamb:

Great and awesome are Your works, Lord God, the Almighty;
righteous and **true are Your ways**, King of the Nations.
4 Who will not fear, Lord, and glorify Your name?
Because You alone are holy,
because all the nations will come and worship before You,
because Your righteous acts have been revealed.

5 After this I looked, and the heavenly sanctuary—the **tabernacle** of testimony—was opened. **6** Out of the **sanctuary** came the seven angels with the seven plagues, dressed in clean, bright linen, with gold sashes wrapped around their chests. **7** One of the four living creatures gave the seven angels seven gold bowls filled

Living Insights

"victory"
Think what the faithful have overcome—the political power of the Antichrist, the religious oppression of the False Prophet, and the economic pressure of the final days.

"harps from God"
This is the only verse that mentions humans playing harps in heaven. So apparently, we'll be doing a lot more than that when we get there.

"true are Your ways"
The fact that these who have endured one persecution after another can still sing this heartfelt affirmation gives God's sovereignty even more weight.

"tabernacle"
Moses had built his tabernacle based on a heavenly model. Here is the original. Imagine the emotion and encouragement this caused in a first-century believer.

"no one could enter"
For the final act of earth's judgment, God sits alone in perfect holiness and sovereignty, fully capable and fully justified to reap His righteous revenge.

"completed"
The seventh trumpet sounded at 11:15. Everything since then has been outside a time frame. Starting with chapter 16, the clock will be ticking again.

with the wrath of God who lives forever and ever. [8] Then the sanctuary was filled with smoke from God's glory and from His power, and **no one could enter** the sanctuary until the seven plagues of the seven angels were **completed**.

End-Times Insight

Music is one earthly enjoyment that God will let us take to heaven with us. Have you been practicing His praises lately?

Word Study

"sanctuary"

The noun *naos* [NAH ahss] is related to the verb *naio* meaning *to dwell*. *Naos* occurs more often in Revelation than in any other New Testament book. This *naos*, not on earth but in heaven, is the place of special blessing and protection for God's people (3:12; 7:15) and the source of judgment on His enemies (11:19; 14:15,17; 15:5-6,8; 16:1,17). The final *naos* is not a structure at all but the actual presence of the Lord and the Lamb in the new Jerusalem (21:22).

Is Armagedon for Real?

REVELATION 16

Most educated people dismiss the idea that Armagedon is a true prophecy about the end of the world. Little by little, this ominous word that had for hundreds of years evoked images of unimaginable, nightmarish horrors, has become little more than a trivial catchword. When Theodore Roosevelt called his last political battle an "armagedon," the world was beginning to embrace the notion that God's end-time imagery was little more than a sanctimonious scare tactic.

On the other hand, the unfortunate Thomas Brightman identified Geneva, Switzerland, as Armagedon, and expected a literal attack from an army both Roman and Catholic that would be defeated by Reformed forces.

As we have seen, John gives us just enough material from his vision to assure us that the prophecies in this chapter are certain. And that fact alone should satisfy our curiosity and solidify our faith. Yes, John's words describe the end of the world in a lurid light. Yet by the unique term *Armagedon* that he uses, we are denied assurance of the place he has in mind. It is often interpreted as Mount Megiddo (Har-Megiddo), but this is uncertain. And this uncertainty is just as well. Christians are not to live in fear of Armagedon, but we are to live with Christ's warning from this chapter, "I am coming like a thief."

How serious should we be about Armagedon? Should we speculate and hope to locate it on the calendar or the globe? Or should we brush it aside as a handy synonym for a decisive battle?

The challenge from studying this chapter is to affirm, "Yes, I believe that an end-of-the-world battle—which is code-named

Armagedon—will happen. I believe it will be part of God's final judgment. This means that I must live my life now, preparing not so much for Armagedon, but for Christ's return for me." We may live through many a stormy blast, but we can rest in God's purposes being accomplished.

Henry Drummond tells of two painters asked to illustrate their concept of rest. The first chose a scene of a still, quiet lake hidden in the mountains. The second put on his canvas a thundering waterfall with a fragile birch tree bending over the foam. At the fork of a branch, almost in reach of the spray, sat a robin on its nest. The first painting actually represents stagnation. Only the second one depicts genuine rest. While the nightmares of Revelation may be approaching even in our day, we may live like the robin nesting above the rapids.

Prayer

Lord God, I know Your coming judgments will be true and just. Help me live with such readiness that when Jesus comes like a thief, I will not be like the one who goes "naked, and they see his shame."

Chapter 16

John's second vision concludes with a great calamity, as the over-advertised clash of Armagedon becomes a first-round knockout.

Then I heard a **loud voice** from the sanctuary saying to the seven angels, "Go and pour out the seven bowls of God's wrath on the earth." 2 The first went and poured out his bowl on the earth, and severely painful sores broke out on the people who had the mark of the beast and who worshiped his image.

3 The second poured out his bowl into the sea. It turned to blood like a dead man's, and **all life** in the sea died.

4 The third poured out his bowl into the rivers and the springs of water, and they **became blood**. 5 I heard the angel of the waters say:

> You are righteous, who is and who was, the Holy One,
>   for You have decided these things.
> 6 Because they poured out the blood of the saints
>   and the prophets,
>   You also gave them blood to drink; **they deserve it**!

7 Then I heard someone from the altar say:

> Yes, Lord God, the Almighty,
>   true and righteous are Your judgments.

Living Insights

"loud voice"

This is none other than the voice of God, acting alone and in full authority over the affairs of men.

"all life"

Without life in the sea, life on land can't last long. These judgments are happening in rapid succession.

"became blood"

Most of these perils, like this one, correspond to the plagues God poured out on Egypt, only magnified to global proportions.

"they deserve it"

This is hard to read, hard to square with a spiritually soft view of God, but this is justice. "They deserve it."

"it is done"

God speaks with the same finality, the same verb tense, as when Jesus declared from the cross, "It is finished."

"three parts"

Another way to say *total ruin*. It's all over but the crying for the devil, the beast, and the false prophet.

8 The fourth poured out his bowl on the sun. He was given the power to burn people with fire, **9** and people were burned by the intense heat. So they blasphemed the name of God who had the power over these plagues, and they did not repent and give Him glory.

10 The fifth poured out his bowl on the throne of the beast, and his kingdom was plunged into darkness. People gnawed their tongues from pain **11** and blasphemed the God of heaven because of their pains and their sores, yet they did not repent of their actions.

12 The sixth poured out his bowl on the great river Euphrates, and its water was dried up to prepare the way for the kings from the east. **13** Then I saw three unclean spirits like frogs coming from the dragon's mouth, from the beast's mouth, and from the mouth of the false prophet. **14** For they are spirits of demons performing signs, who travel to the kings of the whole world to assemble them for the battle of the great day of God, the Almighty.

15 "Look, I am coming like a thief. Blessed is the one who is alert and remains clothed so that he may not go naked, and they see his shame."

16 So they assembled them at the place called in Hebrew Armagedon.

17 Then the seventh poured out his bowl into the air, and a loud voice came out of the sanctuary, from the throne, saying, "**It is done**!" **18** There were lightnings, rumblings, and thunders. And a severe earthquake occurred like no other since man has been on the earth—so great was the quake. **19** The great city split into **three parts**, and the cities of the nations fell. Babylon the Great was remembered in God's presence; He gave her the cup filled with the wine of His fierce anger. **20** Every island fled, and the mountains disappeared. **21** Enormous hailstones, each weighing about a hundred pounds, fell from heaven on the people, and they blasphemed God for the plague of hail because that plague was extremely severe.

Word Study

"deserve"

The Greek adjective *axios* [AHKS ee ahss] means *worthy* or *deserving* and can be used in either a positive or negative sense. The word picture is of a scale where an item on one side should balance with an item on the other side. If it does, it is *worthy*. In Revelation, Christ declares the redeemed worthy of their reward (3:4) and the wicked worthy of theirs (16:6). God is worthy of glory (4:11), and only the Lamb is found worthy to break the seals on the scroll (5:2,4,9,12).

End-Times Insight

*You can pray, you can prod, but some
people will never repent, no matter what.*

Devil in a Red Dress

REVELATION 17

If my interpretation of the prostitute riding the seven-headed monster is correct, then today we are living in a period "between the heads." The five great empires that opposed God's people throughout history no longer exist in their once sweeping scope—Egypt, Assyria, Babylon, Persia, and the Seleucid Empire (whose Antiochus Epiphanes desecrated the temple and outlawed the practice of Judaism). The sixth head, the Roman empire—the reigning world power at the time of John's vision—is also fallen. Only the seventh head is yet to come (Antichrist's kingdom). We are between the era when the city of Rome was queen of world civilization and the short period when "Babylon the Great" will rule.

But the truth symbolized by the prostitute is as powerful now as it was during the height of Rome's splendor. The forces of human civilization are hostile to a living faith in God. In his First Epistle, John taught the same truth this way: "Everything in the world—the lust of the flesh, the lust of the eyes and the pompous pride of life—is not from the Father, but is from the world. And the world is passing away, and its lust, but whoever does God's will remains forever. Children, it is the last hour. And just as you have heard that the Antichrist is coming, so now many antichrists have appeared. By this we know that it is the last hour" (1 John 2:15b–18).

We must choose between the city of Babylon and the city of God. We may go with the flow and allow ourselves to be with the great majority of humanity, enchanted by the great mistress. She is aided by the supernatural workings of the great dragon, Satan. She appears oh so lovely, but hers is a beauty created by hell itself.

In *The City of God,* Augustine warned against this bewitchment: "Perhaps our readers expect us to say something about this so great delusion wrought by the demons; and what shall we say but that men must fly out of the midst of Babylon? For this prophetic precept is to be understood spiritually in this sense, that by going forward in the living God, by the steps of faith, which work by love, we must flee out of the city of this world, which is altogether a society of ungodly angels and men. Yes, the greater we see the power of the demons to be in these depths, so much the more tenaciously must we cleave to the Mediator through whom we ascend from these lowest to the highest places" (18, 18).

The prostitute is offering herself to the people of this age, through the movies, the media, the society page, the sportsfield. Are you keeping your distance, or are you listening, half believing she has something important to say?

Prayer

Lord, I need Your help to keep me from being led astray by the subtle, sinful pleasures of our culture. Strengthen me to be Your faithful follower, that I would gladly die for bearing Your name.

Chapter 17

Preview

John's third vision now begins, painting the events he's just described in an even seedier light.

Then one of the seven angels who had the seven bowls came and spoke with me: "Come, **I will show you** the judgment of the notorious **prostitute** who sits on many waters. 2 The kings of the earth committed sexual immorality with her, and those who live on the earth became drunk on the wine of her sexual immorality." 3 So he carried me away in the Spirit to a desert. I saw a woman sitting on a **scarlet beast** that was covered with blasphemous names, having seven heads and ten horns. 4 The woman was dressed in purple and scarlet, adorned with gold, precious stones, and pearls. She had a gold cup in her hand filled with everything **vile** and with the impurities of her prostitution. 5 On her forehead a cryptic name was written:

> BABYLON THE GREAT
> THE MOTHER OF PROSTITUTES
> AND OF THE VILE THINGS OF THE EARTH

6 Then I saw that the woman was drunk on the blood of the saints and on the blood of the witnesses to Jesus. When I saw her, I was utterly astounded.

Living Insights

"I will show you"
The events of the next few chapters don't come after the earlier visions, but instead tell the same story from a different perspective.

"prostitute"
She represents all that is corrupt in worldly culture—arrogance, autonomy, injustice, and oppression of God's people.

"scarlet beast"
Described just like the beast in 13:1—the Antichrist, carrying the world on the shoulders of raw power and ungodly hatred.

"seven mountains"
The people of John's day would know this as Rome, the city of seven hills. But certainly, that's only part of the interpretation.

"destruction"
Whatever we're to understand from this puzzling prophecy, one thing's for sure: Antichrist's days are numbered.

"hate the prostitute"
History proves that corrupt people will often turn against their own allies, foolishly hastening their own demise.

Word Study

"vile"

The Greek noun *bdel-ugma* [BDEHL oog mah] means *abomination* or *detestable*. The related adjective *bdeluktos* means *detestable* or *vile*; another related term, *bdelugmia*, not used in the New Testament, means *nausea* or figuratively *disgust*. The corresponding verb *bdelussomai* literally means *to feel nause-ated* or *to be sick*, and figuratively to *abhor* or *loath*. In Revelation 17-18, the term *bdelugma* is used not only to describe Babylon (17:4) but is actually part of her name (17:5).

7 Then the angel said to me, "Why are you astounded? I will tell you the secret meaning of the woman and of the beast with the seven heads and the ten horns that carries her. **8** The beast that you saw was, and is not, and is about to come up from the abyss and go to destruction. Those who live on the earth whose names were not written in the book of life from the foundation of the world will be astounded when they see the beast that was, and is not, and will be present again.

9 "Here is the mind with wisdom: the seven heads are **seven mountains** on which the woman is seated. **10** They are also seven kings: five have fallen, one is, the other has not yet come, and when he comes, he must remain for a little while. **11** The beast that was and is not, is himself the eighth, yet is of the seven and goes to **destruction**. **12** The ten horns you saw are ten kings who have not yet received a kingdom, but they will receive authority as kings with the beast for one hour. **13** These have one purpose, and they give their power and authority to the beast. **14** These will make war against the Lamb, but the Lamb will conquer them because he is Lord of lords and King of kings. Those with him are called and elect and faithful."

15 He also said to me, "The waters you saw, where the prostitute was seated, are peoples, multitudes, nations, and languages. **16** The ten horns you saw, and the beast, will **hate the prostitute**. They will make her desolate and naked, devour her flesh, and burn her up with fire. **17** For God has put it into their hearts to carry out His plan by having one purpose, and to give their kingdom to the beast until God's words are accomplished. **18** And the woman you saw is the great city that has an empire over the kings of the earth."

End-Times Insight

Christians must strive daily to be astounded by sin instead of enticed by it.

Come Out, Wherever You Are

Revelation 18

Martin Luther, the great Reformer, became persuaded that the Roman Catholic system of his day was the great harlot of Revelation. He acted on his convictions by bravely leaving the system. He "came out of her," arguing on the basis of Revelation that the complete doom of Catholicism was soon at hand.

Of course, this did not happen. While the corrupt system of his day may have reflected the spirit of Babylon, Babylon is much more wicked and perverse than anything the sixteenth century had to offer. Yet we admire Luther for having the courage of his convictions. We, too, may not live to see Babylon in its final, most appalling form, but just as in Luther's era, the spirit of Babylon is still thriving today. We join the first-century Christians in reading John's exhortation to "come out of her" and are forced to decide how best to obey the divine command.

Revelation 18 makes clear that Babylon can corrupt people in many different ways, showing itself in things like:

- living a luxurious lifestyle at the cost of human misery, lack, and suffering

- indulging in power for power's sake (like the kings)

- assuming that success in trading or transporting goods and similar endeavors provides true security or meaning (like the merchants and mariners)

- believing that ultimate success is found in the arts or domestic life

- allowing false religious concepts to mingle with or replace the Bible's true religion

To the extent that such attitudes or actions have crept into our lives as Christians, we are guilty of committing adultery with Babylon. Studying this chapter should alert us to areas in our own lifestyle that may reflect compromise with the world. When we decide to let go of some area in which we have either wittingly or unwittingly compromised with the corrupt world system, we may take heart from Martin Luther's ringing defense in 1521 before the Diet in the city of Worms: "Your Imperial Majesty and your lordships demand a simple answer. Here it is, plain and unvarnished. Unless I am convicted of error by the testimony of Scriptures...or by manifest reasoning I stand convicted by the Scriptures to which I have appealed and my conscience is taken captive by God's word, I cannot and will not recant anything, for to act against our conscience is neither safe for us, nor open to us. On this I take my stand. I can do no other. God help me. Amen."

Prayer

Lord, I ask You to show me those areas in my own life that are rooted in "Babylon" rather than in You. And help me never be comfortable in the company of those people who would be sad to see her go.

Chapter 18

Preview

After years of enjoying the free rein of sin and selfishness, the mighty city of man succumbs to the awesome reign of God's judgment.

After this I saw another angel with great authority coming down from heaven, and the earth was illuminated by his splendor. 2 He cried in a mighty voice:

It has fallen, Babylon the Great has fallen!
She has become a dwelling for demons,
a haunt for every unclean spirit,
a haunt for every unclean bird,
and a haunt for every unclean and despicable beast.
3 For all the nations have drunk
the wine of her sexual immorality, which brings wrath.
The kings of the earth have committed sexual immorality with her,
and the merchants of the earth have grown wealthy
from her excessive luxury.

4 Then I heard another voice from heaven:

Come out of her, My people,
so that you will not share in her sins,
or receive any of her plagues.
5 For her sins are piled up to heaven,
and God has remembered her crimes.
6 Pay her back the way she also paid,
and double it according to her works.
In the cup in which she mixed,
mix a double portion for her.
7 As much as she glorified herself and lived luxuriously,
give her that much torment and grief.
Because she says in her heart, "I sit as queen;
I am not a widow, and I will never see grief,"
8 therefore her plagues will come **in one day**—
death, and grief, and famine.
She will be burned up with fire,
because the Lord God who judges her is mighty.

9 The kings of the earth who have committed sexual immorality and lived luxuriously with her will weep and mourn over her when they see the smoke of her burning. **10** They stand far off in fear of her torment, saying:

> Woe, woe, the great city,
> Babylon, the mighty city!
> For in a single hour
> your judgment has come.

11 The merchants of the earth will also weep and mourn over her, because no one buys their **merchandise** any longer— **12** merchandise of gold, silver, precious stones, and pearls; fine fabrics of linen, purple, silk, and scarlet; all kinds of fragrant wood products; objects of ivory; objects of expensive wood, brass, iron, and marble; **13** cinnamon, spice, incense, myrrh, and frankincense; wine, olive oil, fine wheat flour, and grain; cattle and sheep; horses and carriages; and human bodies and souls.

> **14** The fruit you craved has left you.
> All your splendid and glamorous things are gone;
> they will never find them again.

15 The merchants of these things, who became rich from her, will stand far off in fear of her torment, weeping and mourning, **16** saying:

Living Insights

"come out of her"
First-century Christians never actually left Rome *en masse*, but they definitely forsook its way of life.

"in one day"
This phrase or its close equivalent—*in one hour*—appears four times in this chapter. All that effort, all gone overnight.

"merchandise"
Clothes and cars, foodstuffs and furniture, perfume and profits—not exactly evil in themselves, unless your life is all wrapped up in them.

"sailors"
Like the others, their sadness is a selfish one—not for Babylon, but for what her loss does to their lives.

"sound of a mill"
Even the ordinary clatter of everyday life is precious when it's no longer heard.

"nobility"
They could have used all that knowledge, ingenuity, and networking for good. Instead, they wasted all God's gifts on themselves.

Woe, woe, the great city,
clothed in fine linen, purple, and scarlet,
adorned with gold, precious stones,
and pearls;
17 because in a single hour such fabulous
wealth was destroyed!

And every shipmaster, seafarer, the **sailors**,
and all who do business by sea, stood far off
18 as they watched the smoke from her burning
and kept crying out: "Who is like the great
city?" 19 They threw dust on their heads and
kept crying out, weeping, and mourning:

Woe, woe, the great city,
where all those who have ships on the sea
became rich from her wealth;
because in a single hour she
was destroyed.
20 Rejoice over her, heaven: saints, apostles
and prophets;
because God has executed your judgment
on her!

21 Then a mighty angel picked up a stone
like a large millstone and threw it into the sea, saying:

In this way, Babylon the great city will be thrown
down violently
and never be found again.
22 The sound of harpists, musicians, flutists, and trumpeters
will never be heard in you again;
no craftsman of any trade
will ever be found in you again;
the **sound of a mill**
will never be heard in you again;
23 the light of a lamp will never shine in you again;
and the voice of a groom and bride
will never be heard in you again.

Word Study

"d e c e i v e"

The Greek verb *planao*
[plahn AH oh] basically
means *to wander* but
was normally used neg-
atively with the mean-
ings *to lead* or *go
astray*. The connotation
of wandering can be
seen in the related
noun *planetes* (English
planet), which means
wanderer. In Revelation
the church at Thyatira
is warned about a
deceiving "Jezebel"
(2:20). The other seven
uses of *planao* refer to
the false prophet
(13:14; 19:20),
Babylon (18:23), and
Satan—the arch
deceiver (12:9;
20:3,8,10).

All this will happen
    because your merchants were the **nobility** of the earth,
    because all the nations were **deceived** by your sorcery,
²⁴ and the blood of prophets and saints,
    and all those slaughtered on earth, was found in you.

End-Times Insight

Constantly remind yourself that
this world is not your home.

Dressed in Righteousness

REVELATION 19

Every human culture celebrates weddings. A near universal custom is for the bride to wear special clothes. She must be at her loveliest on her wedding day. Whether she is Chinese with a red silk dress or American with veil and long-trained white satin gown, the bride always takes extra pains on her wedding day. The bride makes herself ready for her presentation to her bridegroom.

That's why this chapter's portrait of the heavenly wedding between the Lamb-Bridegroom and His church-bride includes the statement, "His wife has prepared herself." Then we are told immediately that the bride's wedding gown is made of "the righteous acts of the saints." Rarely do we consider that the kind of lives we live for Christ now will have an impact on the way the bride of Christ will appear on her wedding day.

On the one hand, only by God's gracious invitation will any human being be a part of that day. ("Blessed are those invited to the marriage feast of the Lamb!") In the language used earlier in Revelation, "These are the ones [who]…washed their robes and made them white in the blood of the Lamb" (7:14). Here is salvation by grace through faith.

On the other hand, enabled by the Spirit of God, Christians have the privilege of doing good works that will be rewarded (1Co 3:12–15). The apostle Paul stated this clearly: "For it is God who works in you both to desire and to work for His good purpose" (Php 2:13).

Elisha Hoffman, a writer of gospel songs, caught this sense of Revelation's teaching with his song beloved by so many Christian congregations but reviled by those that have rejected the scriptural truths undergirding the words. The first stanza focuses on God's grace for conversion, the second on our need to prepare for Christ's return by living holy lives:

> Have you been to Jesus for the cleansing power?
> Are you washed in the blood of the Lamb?
> Are you fully trusting in his grace this hour?
> Are you washed in the blood of the Lamb?
>
> Are you walking daily by the Savior's side?
> Are you washed in the blood of the Lamb?
> Do you rest each moment in the Crucified?
> Are you washed in the blood of the Lamb?

P r a y e r

Lord, thank You for the undeserved invitation to partake in Your wedding feast. Prepare me now for that marvelous day by helping me live a life of faith and obedience while I'm here on this earth.

Chapter 19

Preview

Christ returns to earth in holy triumph, calling His people to a victory dinner, leaving the rest as bird food.

After this I heard something like the loud voice of a vast multitude in heaven, saying:

> Hallelujah!
> Salvation, glory, and power belong to
>   our God,
> ² because His judgments are true and
>   righteous,
> because He has judged the notorious prostitute
> who corrupted the earth with her sexual immorality;
> and He has avenged the blood of His servants that was
>   on her hands.

³ A second time they said:

> Hallelujah!
> Her smoke ascends forever and ever!

⁴ Then the twenty-four elders and the four living creatures fell down and worshiped God, who is seated on the throne, saying:

> Amen! Hallelujah!

⁵ A voice came from the throne, saying:

> Praise our God,
> all you His servants, you who fear Him,
> both small and great!

⁶ Then I heard something like the voice of a vast multitude, like the sound of cascading waters, and like the rumbling of loud thunder, saying:

> Hallelujah—because our Lord God, the Almighty,
> has begun to reign!
> ⁷ Let us be glad, rejoice, and give Him glory,
> because the marriage of the Lamb has come,

Word Study

"shepherd"

The Greek verb
poimaino [poy MIGH
noh] basically means *to
tend or nurture sheep,
to shepherd* but was
often used with the
more forceful and figu-
rative meaning *to rule.*
Revelation 7:17
involves a mixed
metaphor in that "the
Lamb" is going to
"shepherd" the
redeemed. The other
three uses of *poimaino*
in Revelation (2:27;
12:5; 19:15) contain
an allusion to Psalm
2:9, which states that
the Lord's anointed will
shepherd or rule the
nations "with an iron
scepter."

and His wife has prepared herself.
⁸ She was permitted to wear fine linen,
    bright and pure.

For the fine linen represents the righteous acts of the saints.

⁹ Then he said to me, "Write: Blessed are those invited to the marriage feast of the Lamb!" He also said to me, "These words of God are true." ¹⁰ Then I fell at his feet to worship him, but he said to me, "Don't do that! I am a fellow slave with you and your brothers who have the testimony about Jesus. Worship God, because the testimony about Jesus is the spirit of prophecy."

¹¹ Then I saw heaven opened, and there was a white horse! Its rider is called Faithful and True, and in righteousness He judges and makes war. ¹² His eyes were like a fiery flame, and on His head were **many crowns**. He had a name written that **no one knows** except Himself. ¹³ He wore a robe **stained with blood**, and His name is called the Word of God. ¹⁴ The **armies** that were in heaven followed Him on white horses, wearing pure white linen. ¹⁵ From His mouth came a sharp sword, so that with it He might strike the nations. He will

Living Insights

"many crowns"
The dragon had worn seven, the Antichrist ten. The true King arrives wearing more crowns than all of them put together.

"no one knows"
Could it be that there are aspects of Christ's character so infinite that even in our glorified state we may be unable to understand them?

"stained with blood"
Could be Christ's own blood or perhaps the blood of His enemies, the ripe result of the winepress from chapter 14. (See also Isaiah 63:2-4)

"armies"
With Jesus in command, His troops are mere observers, not participants. Their white clothes prove that Christ has conquered all by Himself.

"supper of God"
This gory blood-letting is likely describing the same event as the winepress (14:20) and the seventh bowl judgment (16:17-21).

"thrown alive"
The beast and his prophet make the first splash in the lake of fire, because those who lead others into sin bear a greater responsibility.

shepherd them with an iron scepter. He will also trample the winepress of the fierce anger of God, the Almighty. [16] And on His robe and on His thigh He has a name written:

> KING OF KINGS
> AND LORD OF LORDS

[17] Then I saw an angel standing in the sun, and he cried out in a loud voice, saying to all the birds flying in mid-heaven, "Come, gather together for the great **supper of God**, [18] so that you may eat the flesh of kings, the flesh of commanders, the flesh of mighty men, the flesh of horses and of their riders, and the flesh of everyone, both free and slave, small and great."

[19] Then I saw the beast, the kings of the earth, and their armies gathered together to wage war against the rider on the horse and against His army. [20] But the beast was taken prisoner, and along with him the false prophet, who had performed signs on his authority, by which he deceived those who accepted the mark of the beast and those who worshiped his image. Both of them were **thrown alive** into the lake of fire that burns with sulfur. [21] The rest were killed with the sword that came from the mouth of the rider on the horse, and all the birds were filled with their flesh.

End-Times Insight

Every act of faith and obedience gives
your wedding clothes an added sparkle.

Judgment Day

REVELATION 20

In medieval Europe, powerful church leaders taught ordinary people that life was a temporary pilgrimage, a time of preparing for the eternal state. Everyone understood that they would one day stand before God on judgment day to face His fearful sentence.

The greatest painter ever to depict the judgment was Michelangelo. Many believe that his awesome fresco of the last judgment (painted between 1536–41 for Pope Paul III) in the Sistine Chapel, along with the even more famous frescoes on the chapel's ceiling, is the most important art produced during the Renaissance. I have stood before it in silence myself, awed by its powerful reminder that I, too, will face an eternal Judge one day.

Revelation 20 is another such masterpiece, literary rather than artistic. And despite the difficulties in interpreting portions of the chapter, the central theme is overwhelming. We have misread the chapter if we come away from it unmoved. We must bow before it in silence also.

Sadly, however, many of today's people don't live with that kind of conviction, the awareness that they must live every day in constant preparation for judgment. It's hard to think about a contemporary painter creating a great masterpiece about the coming day of judgment and being taken seriously by the world's artistic community.

In 1834 a young Englishman named Edward Mote wrote a poem he titled "The Gracious Experience of a Christian." One of the stanzas included these words:

I trust His righteous character,
His council, promise, and His power;
His honor and His name's at stake,
To save me from the burning lake.

After American musician William Bradbury wrote a tune for the words in 1863, it became a dearly loved gospel song under the title, "The Solid Rock." Mote's last stanza expresses the heart's desire of Christians everywhere as they realize the seriousness of judgment day:

When He shall come with trumpet sound,
Oh, may I then in Him be found;
Dressed in His righteousness alone,
Faultless to stand before the throne.

Prayer

Lord, I acknowledge that I will one day stand before You as my Judge. May I live in daily anticipation of that frightening yet glorious day, knowing that my faith has found a resting place.

Chapter 20

Preview

The martyrs receive their rich reward, the devil gets his, and the dead rise to meet the righteous Judge.

Then I saw an angel coming down from heaven with the key to the abyss and a great chain in his hand. **2** He seized the dragon, that ancient serpent who is the Devil and Satan, and bound him for a thousand years. **3** He threw him into the abyss, closed it, and put a seal on it so that he would no longer deceive the nations until the thousand years were completed. After that, he must be released for a **short time**.

4 Then I saw thrones, and people seated on them who were given authority to judge. I also saw the souls of those who had been beheaded because of their testimony about Jesus and because of God's word, who had not worshiped the beast or his image, and who had not accepted the mark on their foreheads or their hands. They came to life and reigned with the Messiah for a thousand years. **5** The rest of the dead did not come to life until the thousand years were completed. This is the first resurrection. **6** Blessed and holy is the one who shares in the first resurrection! The second death has no power over these, but they will be priests of God and the Messiah, and they will reign with Him for a thousand years.

Living Insights

"then I saw"
A brief interlude occupies the first ten verses (as in chapters 7 and 10), heightening the suspense before the arrival of Judgment Day.

"short time"
Whatever this passage means, it certainly confirms that although the devil can scare up a lot of trouble, God is not threatened by him.

"deceive the nations"
Whenever the devil is around, he'll always find someone he can trick into doing what he says.

"fire came down"
The final battle between God and Satan turns out to be a nonbattle—all hype and no hope for the devil and his followers.

"great white throne"
Jesus had predicted He would be here, separating "the sheep from the goats," dispensing eternal rewards and punishments (Mt 25:32).

"their works"
One day all our deeds are coming out into the open, even those of the redeemed. Christians saved by faith are not exempt from holy living.

7 When the thousand years are completed, Satan will be released from his prison **8** and will go out to **deceive the nations** at the four corners of the earth, Gog and Magog, to gather them for battle. Their number is like the sand of the sea. **9** They came up over the surface of the earth and surrounded the encampment of the saints, the beloved city. Then **fire came down** from heaven and consumed them. **10** The Devil who deceived them was thrown into the lake of fire and sulfur where the beast and the false prophet are, and they will be tormented day and night forever and ever.

11 Then I saw a **great white throne** and One seated on it. Earth and heaven fled from His presence, and no place was found for them. **12** I also saw the dead, the great and the small, standing before the throne, and books were opened. Another book was opened, which is the book of life, and the dead were judged according to **their works** by what was written in the books.

13 Then the sea gave up its dead, and Death and **Hades** gave up their dead; all were judged according to their works. **14** Death and Hades were thrown into the lake of fire. This is the second death, the lake of fire. **15** And anyone not found written in the book of life was thrown into the lake of fire.

Word Study

"Hades"

The Greek noun *hades* [hah DAYSS] is formed from a root meaning *to see* and a particle that negates it. Thus, the term literally means *that which is not seen* and basically refers to the netherworld, the place where a person's spirit goes after death. In Revelation Hades is always preceded by Death (1:18; 6:8), both of which are defeated at Christ's return (20:13-14). After the resurrection and final judgment, there will be no more death (21:4) and no longer a need for an abode for the dead.

End-Times Insight

How do your plans change for today knowing that your future contains a great white searchlight?

Bright Midnight

REVELATION 21

With all its splendid buildings—temple and palace—the Jerusalem of Solomon was a glittering city on a hill by day. By night, however, even glorious Jerusalem couldn't avoid the unwelcome intrusion of darkness. Only the pale flicker of olive-oil lamps illumined the indoors, while a few scattered torches struggled outside against the night. Before the modern inventions of electric (or gas) light, even the best of cities could be terrifying in the dark.

So you can see how the promise of Revelation 21—that "it will never be night there"—would have had a much more profound impact on John's original readers than it does for us.

But if you think about "night" as being a symbol for the darkness that sin and evil have brought into your own experience, you can sort of begin to sense the desperate hope they felt for God's light to dispel the darkness of their lives. Perhaps you are burdened right now by a broken relationship, a frightening disease, a dreadful habit, or some action done by you or to you that can only be described in the dark, depressing colors and emotions of nighttime. This chapter is a wonderful reminder that God's goodness and greatness will conquer everything that darkens your world, for as sure as the sun rises in the east, "it will never be night there."

A blind preacher, George Matheson, understood this idea more profoundly than most of us ever can. As he reflected on the coming of everlasting light, he penned the following, part of his great poem "O Love That Wilt Not Let Me Go."

O Light that followest all my way,
I yield my flickering torch to Thee
My heart restores its borrowed ray,
That in Thy sunshine's blaze its day
May brighter, fairer be.

O Joy that seekest me through pain,
I cannot close my heart to Thee,
I trace the rainbow through the rain,
And feel the promise is not vain,
That morn shall tearless be.

Prayer

Lord, thank You that in heaven I will be with You forever, You will banish all sin and evil, and there will be no night there. Help me to live today with this picture of coming bliss ever before me.

Chapter 21

Preview

John's third vision ends while overlooking the heavenly city, before his final revelation (starting in verse 9) takes him on the grand tour.

Then I saw a new heaven and a new earth, for the first heaven and the first earth had passed away, and the sea existed no longer. ² I also saw the **Holy City**, new Jerusalem, coming down out of heaven from God, prepared like a bride adorned for her husband.

³ Then I heard a loud voice from the throne:

Look! God's dwelling is with men,
and He will live with them.
They will be His people,
and God Himself will be with them and be their God.
⁴ He will wipe away every tear from their eyes.
Death will exist no longer;
grief, crying, and pain will exist no longer,
because the previous things have passed away.

⁵ Then the One seated on the throne said, "Look! I am making **everything new**." He also said, "Write, because these words are faithful and true." ⁶ And He said to me, "It is done! I am the **Alpha** and the Omega, the Beginning and the End. I will give to the thirsty from the spring of living water as a gift. ⁷ The victor will inherit these things, and I will be his God, and he will be My

Living Insights

"Holy City"
She is obviously the exact opposite of the wicked city Babylon—the difference between inevitable destruction and unending joy.

"12,000 stadia"
It's symbolic for "huge," but a literal measurement would put it at 1,400 miles across, about the distance from Dallas to Los Angeles.

"sanctuary"
The only thing the temple was ever supposed to be was a place to experience God's presence. In heaven, it literally *is* God's presence.

"everything new"
Ever wonder what the earth was like before the Fall? Here's a brand new one, this time with an eternal lifetime guarantee.

"equal"
The city is as tall as it is wide, and as wide as it is deep—a perfect cube— the exact shape of the Old Testament's Holy of Holies.

"honor of the nations"
Not all of man's achievements were selfish and godless. Those inspired by and offered to God will continue to bless Him in eternity.

son. **8** But the cowards, unbelievers, vile, murderers, sexually immoral, sorcerers, idolaters, and all liars—their share will be in the lake that burns with fire and sulfur, which is the second death."

9 Then one of the seven angels, who had held the seven bowls filled with the seven last plagues, came and spoke with me: "Come, I will show you the bride, the wife of the Lamb." **10** He then carried me away in the Spirit to a great and high mountain and showed me the holy city, Jerusalem, coming down out of heaven from God, **11** arrayed with God's glory. Her radiance was like a very precious stone, like a jasper stone, bright as crystal. **12** The city had a massive high wall, with twelve gates. Twelve angels were at the gates; on the gates, names were inscribed, the names of the twelve tribes of the sons of Israel. **13** There were three gates on the east, three gates on the north, three gates on the south, and three gates on the west. **14** The city wall had twelve foundations, and on them were the twelve names of the Lamb's twelve apostles.

15 The one who spoke with me had a gold measuring rod to measure the city, its gates, and its wall. **16** The city is laid out in a square; its length and width are the same. He measured the city with the rod at **12,000** *stadia.* Its length, width, and height are **equal**. **17** Then he measured its wall, 144 cubits according to human measurement, which the angel used. **18** The building material of its wall was jasper, and the city was pure gold like clear glass.

19 The foundations of the city wall were adorned with every kind of precious stone:

> the first foundation jasper,
> the second sapphire,
> the third chalcedony,
> the fourth emerald,

Word Study
"Alpha"

The word *alpha* [AL fah] is the first letter of the Greek alphabet. It occurs three times in Revelation, paired with the last letter of the alphabet as a title for deity: "the Alpha and the Omega." Other phrases that appear along with it interpret its meaning: "the one who is and who was and who is coming" (1:8), "the beginning and the end," (21:6), "the first and the last" (22:13). Jesus and the Father are both God, with the power to start everything and the power to end everything.

²⁰ the fifth sardonyx,
the sixth carnelian,
the seventh chrysolite,
the eighth beryl,
the ninth topaz,
the tenth chrysoprase,
the eleventh jacinth,
the twelfth amethyst.

²¹ The twelve gates are twelve pearls; each individual gate was made of a single pearl. The broad street of the city was pure gold, like transparent glass.

²² I did not see a **sanctuary** in it, because the Lord God the Almighty and the Lamb are its sanctuary. ²³ The city does not need the sun or the moon to shine on it, because God's glory illuminates it, and its lamp is the Lamb. ²⁴ The nations will walk in its light, and the kings of the earth will bring their glory into it. ²⁵ Each day its gates will never close because it will never be night there. ²⁶ They will bring the glory and **honor of the nations** into it. ²⁷ Nothing profane will ever enter it: no one who does what is vile or false, but only those written in the Lamb's book of life.

End-Times Insight

Trouble may sometimes feel like your middle name.
But one day—one day—your troubles will all be over.

Clothes So White, They Sparkle

REVELATION 22

Without doubt, washing clothes is one of the least favorite domestic duties. I've never known anyone who does laundry just for sheer enjoyment. People who wash clothes do so either by necessity or to earn money. People both in the ancient world and in our high-tech society, however, cannot escape the call of the laundry. Dirty clothes do not go away if they are ignored.

Revelation often presents the imagery of clothing, from the risen Christ's glorious garments in chapter 1 to the gaudy harlot's in chapter 17. Yet 7:14 and 22:14 are the only two texts that borrow from the language of the laundry. They speak of two different kinds of washing, better known in the ancient world than in ours. The first verse refers to a single, major laundering. In the ancient world, a heavily soiled robe might be taken to a river, rubbed with lye soap, and scrubbed on the rocks to get all the dirt and stains out. (Doing the laundry was a day-long ordeal for women worldwide until the invention of the electric washing machine.) This is quite a picture for the conversion of the sinner. Persons stained by sin may have their robes made perfectly clean by being washed in the Lamb's blood (7:14).

Revelation 22:14, however, pronounces special blessing on another kind of washing. This is not the washing of conversion but the day-by-day "spot washing" involved in making a clean robe stay that way. Picture a snowy white robe that someone has worn out on the streets. A small splatter of mud may have been kicked up by a careless wagon. Perhaps the wearer spilled food down the front. In such cases, rather than taking the robe down to the river, the spots would be removed at home on a daily basis.

That's the way it is in our spiritual lives. The first question is: Have our robes been laundered in the Lamb's blood? Have we come to Christ for salvation? If the answer is yes, then chapter 22 confronts us with a second question: Do we keep coming to the Lamb so that He may remove the small spots from our robes? Do we come to Christ daily in repentance for the sins we commit because of the world, the flesh, and the devil?

According to the testimony of 22:14, only those who keep coming to the Lamb regularly to "wash their robes" demonstrate that they belong to Him, and so "have the right to the tree of life." And so the closing challenge of Revelation is for us to soberly evaluate our daily lives, to evaluate the genuineness of our original profession of faith in Christ in the light of our fellowship with Him on an ongoing basis.

Prayer

Maranatha! Come, Lord Jesus.

Chapter 22

Preview

The certainty of Christ's glorious return is forever established. Revelation concludes with words that are worth their weight in hope.

Then he showed me the river of living water, sparkling like crystal, flowing from the throne of God and of the Lamb **2** down the middle of the broad street of the city. On both sides of the river was the tree of life bearing twelve kinds of fruit, producing its fruit every month. The leaves of the tree are for **healing the nations**, **3** and there will no longer be any **curse**. The **throne of God** and of the Lamb will be in the city, and His servants will **serve Him**. **4** They will see His face, and His name will be on their **foreheads**. **5** Night will no longer exist, and people will not need lamplight or sunlight, because the Lord God will give them light. And they will reign forever and ever.

6 Then he said to me, "These words are faithful and true. And the Lord, the God of the spirits of the prophets, has sent His angel to show His servants what must quickly take place."

7 "Look, I am coming quickly! Blessed is the one who keeps the prophetic words of this book."

8 I, John, am the one who heard and saw these things. When I heard and saw them, I fell down to worship at the feet of the angel who had shown them to me. **9** But he said to me, "Don't do that! I am a fellow slave with you, your brothers the prophets, and

Living Insights

"healing the nations"
Since healing is not required in heaven, this may simply mean that we will all enjoy the blessing of full health from God's hand.

"curse"
The last of seven things to be banished forever: the sea, death, mourning, crying, pain, darkness—and now this. Total blessing takes its place.

"throne of God"
The Garden of Eden had its own tree and river. But the added presence of God's throne makes this the ultimate paradise.

"serve Him"
Our eternal home is going to be a busy place—finally a chance to serve God with all our energy and passion, without the slightest hint of sin.

"I, Jesus"
He's been letting the angels do a lot of His talking for Him, but three times in this chapter, Christ seals His promise personally.

"I testify"
John already knew this was Scripture he was writing. His parting words are clear: You can take this book all the way to the bank.

Word Study

"forehead"

The Greek noun *meto-pon* [MEH toh pahn] literally means *between the eyes* and is the word for *forehead*. The word occurs only in Revelation, and in each case a mark or seal on the forehead is in view. The name of the woman on the scarlet beast is written on her forehead (17:5). The mark of the beast is taken on the right hand or forehead (13:16; 14:9; 20:4). And God claims ownership of His slaves by sealing them on their foreheads with His name (7:3; 9:4; 14:1; 22:4).

those who keep the words of this book. Worship God." **10** He also said to me, "Don't seal the prophetic words of this book, because the time is near. **11** Let the unrighteous go on in unrighteousness; let the filthy go on being made filthy; let the righteous go on in righteousness; and let the holy go on being made holy."

12 "Look! I am coming quickly, and My reward is with Me to repay each person according to what he has done. **13** I am the Alpha and the Omega, the First and the Last, the Beginning and the End.

14 "Blessed are those who wash their robes, so that they may have the right to the tree of life and may enter the city by the gates. **15** Outside are the dogs, the sorcerers, the sexually immoral, the murderers, the idolaters, and everyone who loves and practices lying.

16 "**I, Jesus**, have sent My angel to attest these things to you for the churches. I am the Root and the Offspring of David, the Bright Morning Star."

17 Both the Spirit and the bride say, "Come!" Anyone who hears should say, "Come!" And the one who is thirsty should come. Whoever desires should take the living water as a gift.

18 **I testify** to everyone who hears the prophetic words of this book: If anyone adds to them, God will add to him the plagues that are written in this book. **19** And if anyone takes away from the words of this prophetic book, God will take away his share of the tree of life and the holy city, written in this book.

20 He who testifies about these things says, "Yes, I am coming quickly."

Amen! Come, Lord Jesus!

21 The grace of the Lord Jesus be with all the saints. Amen.

End-Times Insight

Yes, He is coming soon.
Are you living with the end in sight?